REVISE AQA GCSE
French
REVISION GUIDE

Series Consultant: Harry Smith   Authors: Julie Green and Harriette Lanzer

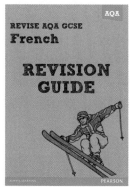

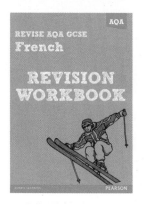

THE REVISE AQA SERIES
Available in print or online

Online editions for all titles in the Revise AQA series are available Summer 2013.

Presented on our ActiveLearn platform, you can view the full book and customise it by adding notes, comments and weblinks.

Print editions

French Revision Guide	9781447941026
French Revision Workbook	9781447941064

Online editions

French Revision Guide	9781447941033
French Revision Workbook	9781447941071

 Audio files
Audio files for the listening exercises in this book can be found at: www.pearsonschools.co.uk/mflrevisionaudio

This Revision Guide is designed to complement your classroom and home learning, and to help prepare you for the exam. It does not include all the content and skills needed for the complete course. It is designed to work in combination with Pearson's main AQA GCSE French 2009 Series.

To find out more visit:
www.pearsonschools.co.uk/aqagcseMFLrevision

D0256058

ALWAYS LEARNING   **PEARSON**

Contents

1-to-1 page match with the **French Revision Workbook** ISBN 9781447941064

LISTENING 21

Audio files

Audio files for the listening exercises in this book can be found at: www.pearsonschools. co.uk/mflrevisionaudio

A small bit of small print

AQA publishes Sample Assessment Material and the Specification on its website. This is the official content and this book should be used in conjunction with it. The questions in *Now try this* have been written to help you practise every topic in the book. Remember: the real exam questions may not look like this.

Target grades

Target grades are quoted in this book for some of the questions. Students targeting this grade should be aiming to get most of the marks available. Students targeting a higher grade should be aiming to get all of the marks available.

Birthdays

You may need to recognise dates in reading and listening questions so learn months and numbers well!

 **Audio files**
Audio files can be found at:
www.pearsonschools.co.uk/mflrevisionaudio

Les anniversaires

J'ai 16 ans.	I am 16 years old.
le premier mars	1st March
le vingt-et-un avril	21st April
le douze mai	12th May
date de naissance (f)	date of birth
Je suis né(e) …	I was born …
Quelle est la date de ton anniversaire?	
When is your birthday?	
Mon anniversaire est (le trois avril).	
My birthday is (3rd April).	

janvier
février
mars
avril
mai
juin

juillet
août
septembre
octobre
novembre
décembre

Alphabet

Comment ça s'écrit?
How do you spell that?

L'alphabet		
A AH	N EN	**Accents**
B BAY	O OH	é accent aigu
C SAY	P PAY	è accent
D DAY	Q COO	grave
E EUH	R ERR	ê circonflexe
F EFF	S ESS	ç cédille
G DJAY	T TAY	– trait d'union
H ASH	U OO	
I EE	V VAY	
J DJEE	W DOOBL-VAY	
K KAH	X EEX	
L ELL	Y EE-GREK	
M EM	Z ZED	

Watch out for the letters in red! Check your alphabet by spelling the English address FAIRVIEW GRANGE.

Worked example

Complete the ID form for this exchange student.
Name: Justine
Age: 15
Birthday: 2nd September

Je me présente. Je m'appelle Justine.
Ça s'écrit J U S T I N E.
J'ai quinze ans. Mon anniversaire est le deux septembre.

EXAM ALERT!

Spellings may crop up in listening passages and the alphabet is an area where students often make mistakes – make sure you don't!

Students have struggled with exam questions similar to this – **be prepared!**

Don't muddle numbers such as **deux** (2) with **douze** (12), or months such as **septembre** (September) with **novembre** (November).

Now try this

Listen to four more exchange students introducing themselves and note down their details.

- Name
- Age
- Birthday

Check that you could give these details about yourself, if asked.

Pets

Use this page to help you talk about pets and use different plural forms.

Les animaux

J'ai ...   I have ...

Je voudrais avoir ...   I would like to have ...

Mon père me permet   My dad
d'avoir ...   lets me have ...

Je n'ai pas de / d'...   I don't have ...

Je n'ai pas d'animal.   I don't have a pet.

un chat   un cheval   un chien   un cochon d'Inde

un lapin   un oiseau   un poisson rouge   une souris

Learning vocabulary

When you learn or revise words, memorise them with the article ('the' or 'a'): that way you'll know if they are masculine or feminine.

	the	a
masculine	le	un
feminine	la	une
plural	les	–

un chien / le chien = masculine

une souris / la souris = feminine

To make most pets plural, add s.

A few are irregular:

un cheval ➡ deux chevaux

un oiseau ➡ deux oiseaux

Words which end in s – don't change!

une souris ➡ deux souris

Worked example

READING | target C

Read the texts.

J'aime les chats mais nous n'avons pas d'animaux parce que ma mère ne les aime pas. **Luc**

Moi, j'adore les animaux. Plus tard, je voudrais être vétérinaire. Chez nous, on a un chien et un oiseau mais on n'a pas de chat ou de lapin. **Jamel**

Moi, je n'aime pas les chiens mais nous avons un chat qui s'appelle Lucie. Elle est mignonne! **Marine**

Nous avons un grand lapin qui s'appelle Maxime. Il est gris et je l'adore. Je voudrais un chien mais mon père ne me le permet pas. **Tom**

Who has a cat? Write **L** (for Luc), **J** (for Jamel), **M** (for Marine) or **T** (for Tom). [M]

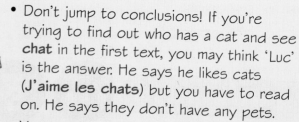

- Don't jump to conclusions! If you're trying to find out who has a cat and see **chat** in the first text, you may think 'Luc' is the answer. He says he likes cats (**J'aime les chats**) but you have to read on. He says they don't have any pets.
- You need to keep looking for **chat** in the other texts to track down the correct answer.
- Watch out for negatives: **on n'a pas ...** = we haven't got ...
- Be careful too of **Je voudrais** = I would like. It indicates what someone **wants**, not what they **have** at the moment.

Now try this

READING | target C

Read the texts again and complete the activity. Who ...

(a) has a parent who doesn't like animals? ☐

(b) has a cute pet? ☐

(c) has a dog? ☐

(d) has a parent who won't let them have a pet? ☐

Physical description

This page will help you to describe yourself and others. Remember to make adjectives agree!

Mon look

Je suis grand(e) / petit(e).	I am tall / small.
Je suis mince / gros(se).	I am thin / fat.
barbe (f)	beard
lunettes (fpl)	glasses
nez (m)	nose
les cheveux marron	brown hair
J'ai un piercing.	I have a piercing.

Il / Elle est de taille moyenne.
He / She is of average height.

J'ai les cheveux courts / longs / mi-longs.
I've got short / long / medium-length hair.

les cheveux bouclés / raides
curly / straight hair

les cheveux roux / noirs / blonds
red / black / blonde hair

J'ai les yeux bleus / gris.
I've got blue / grey eyes.

Il / Elle est beau / belle.
He / She is good-looking.

Je le / la trouve laid(e).
I think he / she is ugly.

Elle est assez jolie.
She is quite pretty.

Irregular adjectives: vieux and beau

 Grammar page 87

	singular		plural	
	masc	fem	masc	fem
old	vieux	vieille	vieux	vieilles
beautiful	beau	belle	beaux	belles

Use vieil and bel in front of masculine singular nouns starting with a vowel or silent h.

Mon père est assez vieux.
My dad is quite old.

Ma sœur est très belle.
My sister is very good-looking.

Worked example

Write a description of yourself.

Je suis assez grand mais un peu trop gros. J'ai les yeux bleus et les cheveux mi-longs et blonds. Ma sœur est jolie mais elle est trop mince.

> This answer uses modifiers like **assez** and **trop**. This makes it more interesting.

> This answer uses the pronoun **lui** (him), which avoids repeating the noun and helps the text flow.

AIMING HIGHER Quand j'étais petite, j'avais les cheveux longs, blonds et bouclés, mais à l'âge de treize ans j'ai découvert un nouveau look! Je suis allée chez le coiffeur et je lui ai demandé de me teindre les cheveux en vert. Quand je suis rentrée à la maison, mes parents étaient vraiment fâchés. Maintenant, j'ai un piercing discret que personne ne peut voir!

Golden rules

① VARY YOUR TENSES – your answer will be more interesting if you write about events which happened in the past too.

② MAKE IT STAND OUT – an unusual twist might make your work stand out from the crowd, e.g. J'ai un piercing discret que personne ne peut voir! (I've got a hidden piercing which nobody can see!)

Now try this

Write a description of yourself or a friend in about 100 words.

Make sure you use:
• modifiers (assez, trop, très)
• correct adjective agreements.

3

Personality

You may need to be able to describe someone's personality. If you are describing real people, remember to be sympa (nice) and sensible (sensitive) to their feelings.

La personnalité

Il / Elle est ...	He / She is ...
aimable	likeable
amical(e)	friendly
amusant(e) / marrant(e)	funny
animé(e)	lively
bavard(e)	chatty
bête	silly
de bonne humeur	good-tempered
de mauvaise humeur	bad-tempered
bruyant(e)	noisy
(dés)agréable	(un)pleasant
drôle	funny / witty
fou / folle	mad
gentil(le)	nice / kind
(im)poli(e)	(im)polite
méchant(e)	mean
paresseux / paresseuse	lazy
pénible	annoying
rigolo	funny
timide	shy
triste	sad

Object pronouns

 Grammar page 92

Use PRONOUNS ('me', 'him', etc.) to avoid repeating nouns.

me	me	us	nous
you	te	you	vous
him / it	le	them	les
her / it	la		

Before vowel / silent h:

me, te, le, la ➡ m', t', l'

Elle me comprend. She understands me.

La mode ne l'intéresse pas. Fashion doesn't interest him / her.

Russell Howard est amusant mais il est parfois méchant!

Worked example

 LISTENING 4   target D

Léa is talking about her best friend Sophie. Which word best describes Sophie?

A noisy
B sociable
C kind

☐ C

Sophie est très gentille mais elle n'aime pas sortir avec ses copains. Elle n'est pas bruyante.

EXAM ALERT!

For this question you need to be able to spot negatives. Many students understand vocabulary but overlook negatives and so fail to answer correctly.

Students have struggled with exam questions similar to this – **be prepared!**

Read carefully: **bruyante** (noisy) is mentioned, but in a negative context – **elle n'est pas ...** (she isn't ...). Don't choose **bruyante** just because you recognise the word.

Now try this

 LISTENING 5   target D

Listen to the rest of the description and choose the **four** correct letters which describe Sophie.

A not keen on fashion
B funny
C sometimes bad-tempered
D lazy
E chatty

F lively
G understanding
H impatient

☐☐☐☐

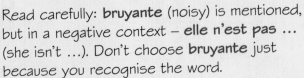

Listen carefully for pronouns: who is **de mauvaise humeur**? Is it Sophie (**elle**) or Léa (**je**)?

Brothers and sisters

This page will prepare you to say lots about your brothers and sisters!

Frères et sœurs

beau-frère (m)	stepbrother
belle-sœur (f)	stepsister
demi-frère (m)	half-brother
demi-sœur (f)	half-sister
jumeaux (mpl) / jumelles (fpl)	twins

Je suis l'aîné(e). — I am the oldest.

J'adore ma petite sœur. — I love my little sister.

Il m'embête. — He annoys me.

Ma belle-sœur est jalouse. — My stepsister is jealous.

Ma grande sœur est mariée / égoïste.
My big sister is married / selfish.

Mon petit frère est toujours embêtant.
My little brother is always annoying.

Mon frère aîné est aimable et compréhensif.
My oldest brother is likeable and understanding.

Using on

- The pronoun on is used a lot in French. It can mean 'we', 'one' or 'you'.
- It takes the same part of the verb as il / elle.

On s'amuse bien ensemble.
We have fun together.

On s'entend bien.
We get on well.

On peut tout se dire.
We can say anything to each other.

On se dispute beaucoup.
We quarrel a lot.

Worked example

SPEAKING

Parle de tes frères et sœurs.

> J'ai deux sœurs qui s'appellent Alice et Wendy. Elles se disputent sans cesse. Je m'entends bien avec Alice parce qu'on s'amuse bien ensemble et on aime la même musique. Cependant, je ne m'entends pas bien avec Wendy parce qu'elle est trop égoïste.

This makes good use of the relative pronoun **qui**, a variety of verb forms **je, elles, elle, on** and opinions + reasons. **But** there is no variety of tenses, which means that this student is unlikely to achieve a higher grade.

AIMING HIGHER

> J'ai un frère et une sœur. Quand j'étais plus jeune, je ne m'entendais pas bien avec mon petit frère parce qu'il était un véritable casse-pieds et je devais m'occuper de lui, mais maintenant on s'entend mieux. Ce weekend, je vais lui apprendre à nager.

This student uses **three tenses**: the **imperfect** to say what his relationship with his brother used to be like, the **present** to compare that with how things are now, and the **future** to say what he's going to do.

Aiming higher

If you are aiming for a top grade, you need to:

✓ include more complex sentences

✓ justify your opinions

✓ use elements such as comparatives (e.g. mieux – better) and indirect pronouns (e.g. lui – him).

Now try this

SPEAKING

Answer these questions about your brothers and sisters. Speak for about one minute.

- Tu as des frères et sœurs? Tu peux les décrire?
- Tu t'entends bien avec tes frères / sœurs? Pourquoi (pas)?
- Comment serait ton frère / ta sœur idéal(e)?

Family

This page will help you talk about your family, even if it's complicated.

La famille

mère — mother
femme — wife
grand-mère — grandmother
père — father
mari — husband
grands-parents — grandparents
grand-père — grandfather
fils — son
fille — daughter

cousin (m) / cousine (f)	cousin
fils / fille unique (m/f)	only child
maman (f)	mum
mère (f)	mother
neveu (m)	nephew
nièce (f)	niece
oncle (m)	uncle
papa (m)	dad
petit(e)-enfant (m/f)	grandchild
tante (f)	aunt

Using ne ... plus (no longer)

Il n'habite plus chez nous.
He doesn't live with us any more.
Il ne reste plus rien.
There isn't anything left (any more).

Il / Elle est ...	He / She is ...
célibataire	single
divorcé(e)	divorced
fiancé(e)	engaged
marié(e)	married
mort(e)	dead
séparé(e)	separated

Note that **beau / belle** means 'step-' or 'in-law':
beau-père (m) stepfather
belle-mère (f) mother-in-law

Worked example

 target B

Read the text.

> Quand j'étais petite, j'habitais avec mes parents, mais ils sont séparés depuis quatre ans alors maintenant j'habite chez ma mère et mon beau-père. Mon beau-père a un fils qui n'habite plus chez nous depuis son mariage l'hiver dernier. La plupart du temps, j'ai de bons rapports avec ma mère. Quelquefois, elle se fâche avec moi et elle m'embête quand elle me pose tout le temps des questions. Elle ne me permet pas de sortir tard le soir, sauf pour aller aux cours de judo. Mon beau-père est sportif - il aime jouer au golf - et je m'entends assez bien avec lui. De temps en temps, il m'aide avec mes devoirs si j'ai des difficultés.

Write **T** (true), **F** (false) or **?** (not in the text).
Margaux now lives with her parents. ⬜ F

Reading exam tips

- Comprehension questions on a reading passage usually follow the ORDER of the text.
- If you can't find the answer to one of the questions in the right place in the text, the correct answer is probably **?** ('not in the text').

This requires knowledge not of key words, but of grammar. It is in the **present** tense: Margaux **now lives** with her parents. So you must ignore references to the past (j'habitais – I lived) and focus on maintenant (now): j'habite (I live).

Now try this

 target B

Read the text again. Answer **T** (true), **F** (false) or **?** (not in the text).

(a) Margaux's stepbrother no longer lives with them. ⬜

(b) Her stepbrother annoys her. ⬜

(c) She doesn't get on with her mum at all. ⬜

(d) She gets on quite well with her stepdad. ⬜

Read the **detail** of each question carefully and look at the **detail** in the text. Don't jump to conclusions!

Friends

You may talk about friends in a speaking assessment so learn some key phrases from this page.

Les copains / copines

ami (m) / amie (f)	friend
copain (m) / copine (f)	friend
petit ami (m) / petite amie (f)	boyfriend / girlfriend
bavarder	to chat
charmant(e)	charming
content(e)	happy
égoïste	selfish
(im)patient(e)	(im)patient
sympa	kind

Je peux compter sur elle / lui. I can count on him / her.

Je le / la connais depuis la maternelle.
I have known him / her since nursery school.

Mon meilleur ami / Ma meilleure amie s'appelle …
My best friend is called …

Question words

qui	who
que	what
où	where
quand	when
quoi	what
quel(le)	which
qu'est-ce que / qui	what
pourquoi	why
combien de	how many / much
comment	how
à quelle heure	at what time

Comment s'appelle votre ami?
What is your friend called?

Qu'est-ce que vous faites?
What do you do?

Worked example SPEAKING

Décris un(e) de tes ami(e)s.

Mon meilleur ami s'appelle Hugo. Je le connais depuis la maternelle. Il est très amusant et très bavard. On s'entend bien ensemble. Je peux compter sur lui quand j'ai un problème.

> This student is accurate **but** hasn't stretched himself to include anything out of the ordinary – he uses basic French, which is fine, but not enough for a top grade.

AIMING HIGHER

J'ai voulu parler de mes copains, parce que ce sont les personnes les plus importantes dans ma vie. J'ai plusieurs amis dans ma classe, mais Marley est mon meilleur ami. Il est très honnête et charmant et je peux tout lui dire. Cet été, nous allons faire un stage de surf au pays de Galles parce que nous adorons faire du sport et après avoir quitté le collège nous voudrions tous les deux aller en Australie pour travailler dans une école de surf.

> The second student has included **past, present** and **future tenses** and the **conditional**, as well as pronouns, different parts of the verb (**je, nous, il**) and a good variety of vocabulary.

CONTROLLED ASSESSMENT

The absence of error does not mean that you will score highly for accuracy, as there must be an attempt to use more complex language and your pronunciation and intonation must be generally good.

Now try this SPEAKING

> Remember to use **different tenses** if you're aiming for one of the highest grades!

Describe one of your friends. Answer the following questions.

- Il / Elle est comment?
- Parle de ce que tu aimes et n'aimes pas.
- Décris quelque chose que vous avez fait ensemble.
- Parle de quelque chose que vous allez faire ensemble.

7

Daily routine

You will need to understand times in the 12-hour clock for tasks on daily routine.

Ma routine quotidienne

Le matin / soir …	In the morning / evening …
L'après-midi …	In the afternoon …
tous les jours	every day
le weekend	at the weekend
je me lève	I get up
je me douche	I shower
je quitte la maison	I leave the house
je vais au collège	I go to school
je prends le bus	I take the bus
je rentre à la maison	I return home
je dîne en famille	I have dinner with my family
je fais mes devoirs	I do my homework
je me couche	I go to bed
je fais la grasse matinée	I sleep in

12-hour clock

à = at
avant = before
après = after

environ = about
(à deux heures environ)

deux heures | deux heures cinq | deux heures et quart

deux heures et demie | trois heures moins le quart | trois heures moins dix

Worked example

READING **target B**

Read the text.

> Les jours d'école, le matin, je me lève à sept heures et je me douche immédiatement. Dix minutes plus tard, je prends mon petit déjeuner. Je mange une tartine avec du miel et je bois un chocolat chaud avant de quitter la maison à sept heures et demie. Mon frère et moi, nous allons au collège en vélo, mais j'y vais avec mes copines et lui avec ses copains. On n'y va jamais ensemble. S'il pleut, nous prenons le car de ramassage qui passe à sept heures vingt. À midi, nous mangeons à la cantine et le soir, nous dînons avec nos parents, puis nous faisons nos devoirs et je tchate en ligne avec ma copine. Nous nous couchons à neuf heures et demie.

Write the correct letter in the box.

At ten past seven, Nina …

A gets up **B** showers **C** has breakfast C

EXAM ALERT!

In multiple-choice questions, you really do have to understand all the text so as not to get misled.

Here, all the items in the choices are in the text, but you have to work out the meaning behind them in order to get the correct answer.

> Students have struggled with exam questions similar to this – **be prepared!**

Make sure you read carefully to find out **who** is doing the various actions:

je = I   nous = we   il = he

Now try this

READING **target B**

Read the text again and write the correct letter in each box.

1 Nina has breakfast …
   A at half past seven   **B** on her way to school   **C** before leaving home ☐

2 She cycles to school …
   A with her friends   **B** with her brother and his friends   **C** alone ☐

3 On a wet day she leaves for school …
   A at seven o'clock   **B** at twenty past seven   **C** in the car ☐

Be careful:
car = coach

4 In the evening Nina's brother …
   A chats to his friend online   **B** does homework with his parents   **C** does homework ☐

Breakfast

This page will help you talk about breakfast in the present and in the past.

Le petit déj(euner)

Pour le petit déjeuner je bois ...	For breakfast I drink ...
du thé	tea
du café	coffee
du jus d'orange	orange juice
du chocolat chaud	hot chocolate
Je ne bois pas de lait.	I don't drink milk.

Je mange ...	I eat ...
des céréales (fpl)	cereals
des crêpes (fpl)	pancakes
du pain (m)	bread
un croissant	a croissant
de la confiture	jam
des fraises (fpl)	strawberries
des framboises (fpl)	raspberries
un œuf	an egg
un pamplemousse	a grapefruit
du jambon	ham
Je ne mange rien.	I don't eat anything.
Je suis pressé(e).	I am in a hurry.

Before and after

- AVANT DE + infinitive = before doing something

  Avant d'aller au collège, je mange des toasts. Before going to school, I eat some toast.

- APRÈS AVOIR + past participle = after doing something

  Après avoir mangé le petit-déj, je suis allé au collège. After eating breakfast, I went to school.

J'adore les céréales et le jus d'orange.

Worked example

Qu'est-ce que tu manges au petit déjeuner?

Pour le petit déjeuner, je mange des céréales avec du lait et je bois un jus d'orange.

AIMING HIGHER Ce matin, j'ai mangé des céréales et du pain beurré avec de la confiture à la framboise. Le weekend, si on a du temps, on fait des crêpes. J'adore ça. Je les mange avec du sucre mais ma sœur les préfère avec des tranches de banane et de la confiture et avec tout ça de la crème fraîche! Je trouve ça dégoûtant!

Aiming higher

Here are four ways to improve your answers:

1. Add an OPINION: C'est assez ennuyeux mais vraiment important. (It's quite boring but really important.)

2. Include a TIME EXPRESSION: toujours (always), quelquefois (sometimes), de temps en temps (now and again).

3. Add a CONDITIONAL: Le petit déjeuner de mes rêves serait ... (The breakfast of my dreams would be ...)

4. Use the PLUPERFECT: Hier, je me sentais malade en classe parce que je n'avais rien mangé avant d'aller à l'école. (Yesterday I felt ill in class because I had not eaten before I went to school.)

Now try this

Use points 1–4 above to prepare answers to these questions.

- Qu'est-ce que tu manges / bois pour le petit déjeuner?
- Quel serait le petit déjeuner de tes rêves?
- Selon toi, c'est important, le petit déjeuner?

Eating at home

Make your sentences longer by adding a connective BUT make sure it makes sense.
Don't repeat it too often OR use the wrong one BECAUSE that would be a shame!

Manger à la maison

bifteck (m)	steak
casse-croûte (m)	snack
déjeuner (m)	lunch
dîner (m)	dinner
fromage (m)	cheese
légumes (mpl)	vegetables
pâtes (mpl)	pasta
plat cuisiné (m)	ready meal
poisson (m)	fish
pomme de terre (f)	potato
repas du soir (m)	evening meal
riz (m)	rice

de la salade

des frites (fpl)

de la viande

saucisses (fpl)	sausages
viande (f)	meat
yaourt (m)	yoghurt

Worked example

Write about what you normally eat at home.

Mon casse-croûte préféré, c'est un
sandwich grillé. On fait un sandwich
avec du jambon et du fromage puis
on le fait griller. Je le mange avec du
ketchup! C'est délicieux!

AIMING HIGHER Chez nous, on mange quand on a
faim! Par exemple, hier, ma sœur a
mangé du bifteck avec des pommes
de terre à quatre heures après
être rentrée de l'école, mais moi,
je ne suis pas arrivé à la maison
avant cinq heures et demie et il ne
restait plus rien dans le frigo. Donc
j'ai dû manger un plat cuisiné du
congélateur parce que mes parents
n'étaient pas allés au supermarché.

This is a good response but to
get a higher grade it would need
to use more than one tense.

This response deserves a higher grade
because it uses **connectives** such as
quand, avec, donc, parce que. It also uses
the **perfect** tense of a modal verb (j'ai
dû manger) and an **imperfect** tense (il ne
restait plus rien), as well as the **present**
tense and a variety of structures.

CONTROLLED ASSESSMENT

In controlled assessment writing tasks, stick
to the 200-word limit. Students who write less
than this cannot aim for the higher grades, and
students who write much more than this often
introduce mistakes.

Now try this

Write about 100 words on your eating habits at home.

- Tu manges en famille le soir?
- Qu'est-ce que tu aimes manger le plus?
- Qui fait la cuisine chez toi?
- Décris ton repas idéal.

Here are some connectives you could use:

et	and	(même) si	(even) if
ou	or	alors	then
mais	but	aussi	also
donc	so / therefore	quand	when
car	because	pendant que	whilst
parce que	because	comme	as

Eating in a café

You may already know lots of food vocabulary, but watch out for false friends, for example les chips = crisps!

Manger au café

une baguette   une bière   un café au lait   une côtelette

des frites (fpl)   une omelette   une glace (à la vanille)   un jus de fruit

une limonade   du gâteau au chocolat   un poulet   une salade verte

un sandwich au jambon   de la soupe   une tarte au citron   un vin rouge

Using vouloir
Grammar page 99

PRESENT

je veux	I want
tu veux	you want
il / elle / on veut	he / she / one wants
nous voulons	we want
vous voulez	you want
ils / elles veulent	they want

Je veux manger.   I want to eat.

Nous voulons aller au café.
We want to go to the café.

PERFECT
j'ai voulu = I wanted
IMPERFECT
je voulais = I used to want
FUTURE
je voudrai = I will want
CONDITIONAL
je voudrais = I would like

Worked example
LISTENING 6   target E

What does Mélissa order? Listen and write the correct letter.

A White wine, strawberry tart and cream
B Red wine and lemon tart
C White wine and lemon tart

☐ C

– Qu'est-ce que vous désirez?
– Euh ... je voudrais un vin blanc.
– Et avec ça?
– Une tarte au citron.
– Avec de la crème?
– Non, merci.

Listening strategies

People sometimes CHANGE THEIR MINDS, so don't assume they are ordering the first item mentioned or that every item of food you hear is relevant. Make sure you listen carefully to the WHOLE DIALOGUE.

Listen for phrases such as **non, merci**, which tells you that someone does not want what is on offer. In Now Try This, listen out for **je regrette** (I'm sorry), which might tell you that something is not available.

Now try this
LISTENING 7   target E

Listen to the whole recording. What do Olivier and Adèle order? Write the correct letter.

Olivier
A Juice, omelette with salad
B White coffee, omelette with salad
C White coffee, croissant with chips   ☐

Adèle
A Mineral water and ice cream
B Chocolate cake and mineral water
C Chocolate cake and fruit juice   ☐

Eating in a restaurant

You might need to understand opinions about restaurants as well as what you eat in them!

Manger au restaurant

une serviette
une cuillère
un verre
une fourchette
une assiette
un couteau

apéritif (m)	pre-dinner drink
boisson (f)	drink
crudités (fpl)	raw chopped vegetables
escargot (m)	snail
fruits de mer (mpl)	seafood
gâteau aux cerises (m)	cherry cake
haricots verts (mpl)	green beans
saumon (m)	salmon
hors d'œuvre (m)	starter
plat (du jour) (m)	dish (of the day)
pourboire (m)	tip
self-service / self (m)	self-service restaurant

Saying 'there'

Grammar page 93

Use y to say 'there' in French.
It replaces à / au / à la / à l' / aux + a noun.

Je vais au café.	I'm going to the café.
➡ J'y vais.	I'm going there.
Je joue au football.	I play football.
➡ J'y joue.	I play it. (football)

IDIOMS WITH Y

Il y a deux cafés.	There are two cafés.
Il y a trois jours.	Three days ago.
On y va!	Let's go!
Allons-y!	Let's go!
Ça y est.	That's it!

Nous y allons pour des fêtes.
We go there for special occasions.

Worked example

LISTENING 8 · target D

Listen. Who says the following? Write **C** (for Clément), **N** (for Nadia) or **M** (for Matthieu).

I really like going to restaurants. ☐ C

– D'abord, Clément. Tu manges souvent au restaurant?

– J'aime bien aller au restaurant mais c'est souvent cher. J'y vais pour les fêtes, par exemple on y est allés le weekend dernier pour l'anniversaire de ma mère. C'était génial!

EXAM ALERT!

Sometimes students struggle when they have to distinguish between likes and dislikes.

Don't jump to conclusions as soon as you hear a key word, but wait to see if there is an opinion accompanying it.

Listen carefully for the names before each speaker in listening tasks like this – the speaker's name is crucial to getting the correct answer.

Students have struggled with exam questions similar to this - **be prepared!**

Now try this

LISTENING 9 · target D

Listen to the whole recording. Who says the following? Write **C** (for Clément), **N** (for Nadia) or **M** (for Matthieu).

(a) I like small restaurants. ☐

(b) I go on special occasions. ☐

(c) I don't like restaurants. ☐

(d) I don't like self-service restaurants. ☐

You need to listen to the **whole passage** in this sort of listening task, as sometimes the answers are not what you think. One speaker says they go to self-service restaurants with friends, but then adds that they don't like going there. Identifying expressions like **n'aime pas** is key.

Healthy eating

Learn some key phrases from this page to talk about healthy eating.

Manger sainement

activité physique (f)	physical activity
alimentation saine (f)	healthy food
eau minérale (f)	mineral water
boissons sucrées (fpl)	sugary drinks
matières grasses (fpl)	fatty foods
nourriture bio (f)	organic food
en bonne forme	fit
en bonne santé	in good health
bon(ne) pour la santé	good for your health
mauvais(e) pour la santé	bad for your health
équilibré(e)	balanced
gras(se)	fatty, greasy
végétarien(ne)	vegetarian
éviter	to avoid
faire un régime	to be on a diet

Present tense -ir verbs

Grammar page 96

grossir	to put on weight
je grossis	I put on weight
tu grossis	you put on weight
il / elle / on grossit	he / she / one puts on weight
nous grossissons	we put on weight
vous grossissez	you put on weight
ils / elles grossissent	they put on weight

- choisir — to choose
- finir — to finish
- maigrir — to lose weight

Je choisis des légumes.

Worked example

READING · target B

Read the text.

> **Alizée** J'adore les gâteaux mais je ne grossis pas parce que je fais beaucoup d'activité physique.
>
> **Sébastien** Pour moi, la nourriture saine est très importante. Je mange beaucoup de fruits, de légumes … Je suis végétarien depuis deux ans.
>
> **Farid** Moi, je crois qu'on doit boire beaucoup d'eau. J'en bois au moins un litre par jour et j'évite les boissons sucrées.
>
> **Célia** Le sport n'a aucune importance pour moi – je ne suis pas en bonne forme mais en générale j'aime l'alimentation saine et j'évite la nourriture qui est mauvaise pour la santé.

Who makes the following statement? Write **A** (for Alizée), **S** (for Sébastien), **F** (for Farid) or **C** (for Célia).

I don't eat meat. ⟦S⟧

Often you are not looking for direct translations in this kind of task, but the same meaning phrased differently. Sébastien doesn't say **Je ne mange pas de viande** (I don't eat meat), but he does say **Je suis végétarien** which means the same thing.

Aiming higher

✓ Look online for forums and articles about any of the subjects you are revising – see how much you can understand of authentic texts to give you confidence in the reading exam.

✓ The more vocabulary you have revised, the easier you will find this kind of task.

Now try this

READING · target B

Read the text again and complete the activity.
Who makes the following statements? Write the correct letter in each box.

(a) I avoid unhealthy drinks. ☐

(b) I'm not interested in exercise. ☐

(c) I have a sweet tooth. ☐

(d) I do a lot of exercise. ☐

Health issues

Health problems may crop up in listening or reading exams, so learn the vocabulary carefully!

Problèmes de santé

comprimé (m)	tablet
maladie (f)	illness
médecin (m)	doctor
obésité (f)	obesity
poumons (mpl)	lungs
toxicomane (m/f)	drug addict
accro	addicted
alcoolique	alcoholic
en bonne santé	healthy
cassé(e)	broken
fatigué(e)	tired
malade	ill
aller mieux	to feel better
désintoxiquer	to detox
prendre un médicament	to take medicine
rester au lit	to stay in bed
J'ai mal à la tête.	My head hurts.
J'ai sommeil.	I feel sleepy.
J'ai vomi.	I was sick.
Je renonce à l'alcool.	I'm giving up alcohol.

Adverbs

Grammar page 91

Adverbs describe verbs: walk QUICKLY, read SLOWLY.

In French, most adverbs are formed by adding -ment to the feminine form of the adjective.

adverbs

- pire — worse
- lentement — slowly
- rapidement — rapidly
- mieux — better
- heureusement — happily / fortunately
- mal — badly
- seulement — only
- bien — well
- régulièrement — regularly
- vraiment — really
- vite — quickly

Worked example

WRITING

Write about what you think are the most serious health problems for young people.

Le problème le plus grave de nos jours, c'est l'alcool. La première fois que j'ai bu de la bière, je me suis senti malade et j'ai vomi. L'alcool peut rapidement donner confiance. Beaucoup de jeunes achètent généralement des canettes au supermarché puis ils en boivent.

AIMING HIGHER Presque tous mes copains ont commencé à boire de l'alcool régulièrement. Mes copains ne remarquent pas quand ils ont trop bu et ils deviennent agressifs. Moi, je n'aime pas l'alcool et quelquefois ils se sont moqués de moi. Mon ami avait renoncé à l'alcool mais c'était vraiment impossible et après un mois il a recommencé. Je crois qu'il en est accro.

This is a good response because it includes **adverbs** (rapidement, généralement) and phrases in the **perfect** tense (j'ai bu, je me suis senti). The student also uses the 3rd person plural (**ils boivent**) to avoid using **je** all the time.

- To gain an even higher grade, this student includes more **complex phrases** such as **ont commencé à boire** (began to drink) and **il en est accro** (he's addicted to it).

- He also uses a **pluperfect** tense (**il avait renoncé à l'alcool** – he had given up alcohol) and a reflexive verb in the **perfect** tense (**ils se sont moqués de moi** – they made fun of me).

Now try this

WRITING

Write about your views on alcohol and your own experiences. Adapt phrases from the texts above.

Remember to include at least **three** tenses if you want to aim for the very top grades.

Health problems

Use this page to become familiar with higher level phrases associated with health problems.

Problèmes de santé

cœur (m)	heart
crise cardiaque (f)	heart attack
douleur (f)	pain
drogue (f)	drugs
fumeur (m) / fumeuse (f)	smoker
habitude (f)	habit
mauvaise santé (f)	bad health
tabac (m)	tobacco
tabagisme (m)	addiction to smoking
dangereux / dangereuse	dangerous
arrêter de fumer	to stop smoking
dormir	to sleep
se sentir	to feel
tousser	to cough
tuer	to kill
vivre	to live
Je me détends.	I relax.
Je suis malade.	I'm ill.
Je ne réussis pas.	I don't succeed.

Aiming higher

Try to include some higher level phrases in your work:

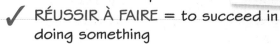

✓ Use DEPUIS to say how long you've been doing something for.
  Je fume depuis deux ans.
  I've been smoking for two years.

✓ ESSAYER D'ARRÊTER = to try to stop
  After de, the second verb is in the infinitive.
  J'ai essayé d'arrêter.
  I've tried to stop.

✓ RÉUSSIR À FAIRE = to succeed in doing something
  After à, the second verb is in the infinitive.
  Je ne réussis pas à arrêter.
  I can't stop. (Literally: I'm not succeeding in stopping.)

Worked example   LISTENING 10   target C

Listen. Write **A** (for Alain), **F** (for Freya) or **G** (for grandad).
Who can't stop smoking?   A

Ici Alain. Je fume depuis cinq ans. Je m'y suis habitué et ... ben ... j'ai essayé plusieurs fois d'arrêter mais je ne réussis jamais. Dès que quelqu'un m'offre une cigarette ... voilà ... je recommence.

• Read the **rubric** and the **question** before you listen – here you can get one step ahead by knowing it is going to be about smoking and involves one of three people.

• The start of the text is all in the 'I' form, **je**, and you already know that Alain is doing the talking, so the statement refers to himself.

Now try this   LISTENING 11   target C

Listen to the whole extract and write **A** (for Alain), **F** (for Freya) or **G** (for grandad).
Who ...
(a) is often ill? ☐
(b) thinks cigarettes are damaging their health? ☐
(c) is totally against smoking? ☐
(d) will never smoke in front of their family? ☐

Relationship plans

Married? Single? Be prepared to say something in French about your relationship plans!

Projets de mariage

amour (m)	love
bague (f)	ring
femme (f)	wife
fiançailles (fpl)	engagement
mari (m)	husband
noces (fpl)	wedding
partenaire idéal(e) (m/f)	ideal partner
petit copain / ami (m)	boyfriend
petite copine / amie (f)	girlfriend
célibataire	single
heureux / heureuse	happy
épouser	to marry
se séparer	to separate

tomber amoureux / amoureuse de
to fall in love with

Je veux me marier.
I want to get married.

Je veux avoir des enfants.
I want to have children.

Mes parents sont divorcés.
My parents are divorced.

Expressing opinions

In your speaking assessment, try to use a range of expressions to give your opinions and reactions:

C'est triste.	It's sad.
C'est mieux.	It's better.
Ce n'est pas grave.	It's not serious.
Ce n'est pas juste.	It's not fair.
C'est la honte!	It's embarrassing!
Ça me fait peur.	It frightens me.
À mon avis / Selon moi …	In my opinion …
Je crois que …	I think that …
Ce serait bon si …	It would be good if …
Je ne suis pas d'accord.	I don't agree.

Je crois que plus tard, je veux me marier.

Worked example

Veux-tu te marier?

Je veux tomber amoureuse. Je veux trouver un petit copain riche. Je veux que mon fiancé m'achète une bague et je veux me marier. Plus tard, je voudrais avoir des enfants et vivre heureuse.

This is a good response. The student uses the **present** tense and the **conditional** (je voudrais avoir – I would like to have). She also makes accurate use of **je veux** + infinitive (I want to …).

AIMING HIGHER

Moi, je ne veux pas me marier parce que je ne veux pas avoir d'enfants. Si on veut en avoir, il faut se marier à mon avis. Mes parents sont divorcés. Ma mère ne me permet pas de rendre visite à mon père – ce n'est pas juste. Plus tard, je voyagerai et je travaillerai pour Médecins Sans Frontières – ce sera plus facile si je suis célibataire.

To get a higher grade, this student uses more complex structures: **Si on veut en avoir** (If you want to have them) and **Ma mère ne me permet pas de rendre visite à …** (My mother doesn't allow me to visit …). He also uses the **future** tense: **je voyagerai** (I will travel) and **je travaillerai** (I will work).

Now try this

Prepare answers to these questions. Speak for about 30 seconds.

- Veux-tu te marier?
- Veux-tu avoir des enfants?

Make sure you try to use at least **three tenses** and include a few more **complex structures**.

Social issues

Use this page to make sure you can discuss some common social issues in French.

Des questions sociales

chrétien(ne) (m/f)	Christian
enlèvement (m)	kidnapping
enquête (f)	enquiry
jugement (m)	judgement
juif / juive (m/f)	Jew
mosquée (f)	mosque
musulman(e) (m/f)	Muslim
organisation caritative (f)	charitable organisation
personnes défavorisées (fpl)	disadvantaged people
sida (m)	AIDS
travail bénévole (m)	charity work
agir	to act
il s'agit de …	it's a question of …
coupable	guilty
déprimé(e)	depressed
illégal(e)	illegal
SDF (sans domicile fixe)	homeless

Relative pronouns

Grammar page 94

qui = who / that

que = which / that / whom

où = where

C'est nous qui devrions persuader …
It's us who should persuade …

C'est quelque chose que tout le monde peut faire.
It's something that everyone can do.

Les pays où on a besoin d'aide.
The countries where they need help.

Worked example

READING   target B

Read this extract from a text.

> À mon avis, c'est nous qui devrions persuader les hommes politiques de faire quelque chose. On devrait leur envoyer des lettres et des e-mails.

A	Lobbying the government
B	Raising money for poor countries
C	Helping combat health issues
D	Problems of religion

Choose the correct title for the text from the list A–D. ☐ A

Reading strategies

- Look for COGNATES (words similar to English words or other French words), e.g. you may not understand les hommes politiques, but you know that hommes means 'men' and politiques looks like 'politics', so homme politique must be 'politician'.
- You won't always find the DIRECT TRANSLATION of the word you're looking for. You may not know the French for 'lobbying the government', but think about what you do if you lobby someone – you send them letters and emails. You'll find envoyer des lettres et des e-mails in the text.

Now try this

READING   target B

Read these texts. Choose a title for each text from A–D above.

1   Il faut absolument combattre le SIDA et d'autres maladies graves. On devrait vendre moins cher les médicaments aux pays en voie de développement où on a besoin d'aide.

☐

2   Si tout le monde travaillait ensemble et discutait et montrait de la tolérance, il y aurait moins de problèmes, par exemple entre les chrétiens, les juifs et les musulmans.

☐

Social problems

You may meet more complex vocabulary in the Higher paper, so learn it well if you're aiming high!

Des problèmes sociaux

argent (m)	money
chômage (m)	unemployment
dette (f)	debt
droits de l'homme (mpl)	human rights
égalité (f)	equality
faim (f)	hunger
immigré(e) (m/f)	immigrant
libertés civiques (fpl)	civil liberties
manifestation (f)	demonstration
pauvreté (f)	poverty
racisme (m)	racism
réfugié(e) (m/f)	refugee
responsabilité (f)	responsibility
sans-abris (mpl/fpl)	homeless people
arrêter	to stop
brutaliser	to ill-treat, to bully
combattre	to combat

Conditional of modal verbs

You use the conditional of modal verbs to say what COULD and SHOULD be done or what you WOULD like.

verb	stem	conditional
devoir	devr-	je devrais (I should)
pouvoir	pourr-	je pourrais (I could)
vouloir	voudr-	je voudrais (I would like)

Modal verbs are followed by an infinitive:

On devrait faire quelque chose.
We should do something.

Je voudrais organiser une manifestation. I would like to organise a demonstration.

Worked example READING target B

Read the text.

> À mon avis, le gouvernement ne fait pas assez pour combattre le vandalisme.
>
> Je pense aussi que les pays riches du monde pourraient donner plus d'argent aux pays pauvres. Cependant, ils donnent souvent des médicaments à ces pays. Pour arrêter la pauvreté, nous en Grande-Bretagne devrions organiser plus de manifestations et de grands évènements télévisés – nous ne faisons pas beaucoup. Cependant, les jeunes dans mon lycée ont récemment fait une course à vélo et ont collecté de l'argent pour aider les pays en voie de développement.

What is Eva's opinion of the government? Write **P** (positive), **N** (negative) or **P/N** (both positive and negative). N

To find Eva's opinion, look for 'government' in the text. The text says that the government **ne fait pas assez** (does not do enough). The **ne ... pas** tells you this is a **negative** opinion.

Little words

Make sure you take notice of 'little' words because they can affect the meaning of a sentence:

cependant	however
plus de	more
souvent	often
pas assez	not enough

Now try this READING target B

Read the rest of the passage above. What is Eva's opinion of a–c? Write **P** (positive), **N** (negative) or **P/N** (both positive and negative).

(a) Rich countries' actions ☐   **(b)** British people ☐   **(c)** Young people in her school ☐

Hobbies

Do your research on hobbies BEFORE your writing assessment. Look up any words in advance and check you are confident in using them.

Les passe-temps

J'aime ...   I like ...

regarder la télé   jouer aux échecs   écouter de la musique

lire   faire les magasins   faire de la natation

faire du patinage   bavarder avec mes amis   jouer de la guitare

Likes and dislikes

aimer ♥	
adorer ♥♥	+ infinitive
détester ✗	
préférer ♥	

J'adore danser. I love dancing / to dance.

Je déteste faire du patinage.
I hate going ice skating.

Je préfère rencontrer mes amis.
I prefer meeting my friends.

Other opinions:

Je suis fan de sport / musique.
I am a fan of sport / music.

Le sport ne m'intéresse pas.
I am not interested in sport.

Worked example

Write about your hobbies.

J'aime écouter de la musique et regarder la télé. Le soir, je joue de la guitare ou je vais au club des jeunes. Je déteste faire mes devoirs, mais c'est nécessaire!

Use **ou** (or) and **et** (and) to list two activities – but don't keep adding **ou** and **et** to make it into a long list. Try instead to use a variety of tenses and forms (**je**, **il**, etc.)!

AIMING HIGHER

Si j'ai le temps, j'aime lire, surtout des livres d'aventure. Quand j'étais plus jeune, je jouais du piano chaque soir, mais maintenant je préfère bavarder avec mes amis ou aller au club de jeunes. Le weekend prochain, nous irons à un festival de musique ensemble et j'espère qu'il ne pleuvra pas parce qu'on va dormir sous des tentes.

- Use **si** (if) and **quand** (when) to make sentences more interesting.
- This student shows off his knowledge of verbs by making accurate use of **three tenses**: **present** (what he likes), **imperfect** (what he used to do) and **future** (what he will do next weekend).

Now try this

What do you do in your free time? Write about 200 words.

- Describe your likes and dislikes.
- Give details of a hobby you used to do.
- Explain how your hobbies have changed.
- Write about your plans for next weekend.

Sport

When you are talking about sports, make sure you get du, de la, de l' and des correct.

Le sport

Je suis sportif / sportive. I'm sporty.

Je joue / jouais …
I play / used to play …

au basket

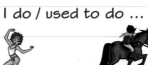
au tennis

Je fais / faisais …　I do / used to do …

du vélo　　de la danse　　de l'équitation

de l'escalade　de la gymnastique　du patin à roulettes

de la voile

du ski nautique

des sports d'hiver

To play / do sports

JOUER + À + sport / game:

Je joue au football.　I play football.

Je joue aux cartes.　I play cards.

FAIRE + DE with other sports:

Je fais de la natation.　I swim.

une / deux fois par semaine
once / twice a week

tous les samedis
every Saturday

Worked example · READING · target **C**

Read the text.

> J'aime le sport. Quand j'étais petit, je jouais au foot. Je m'entraînais deux fois par semaine et le weekend, on jouait contre un autre club. Une fois, on a gagné le championnat – c'était incroyable! Maintenant, mon sport préféré, c'est le judo et j'en fais tous les jeudis. Cet été, pendant les grandes vacances, je vais faire du ski nautique pour la première fois. J'aimerais aussi faire du ski parce que je n'en ai jamais fait et je voudrais bien apprendre. Paul, 16 ans

Read this sentence. Write **T** (true), **F** (false) or **?** (not in the text).

Paul says he trains twice a week at the moment.　F

Past, present and future

- For PAST activities, look for words in the imperfect tense (e.g. étais) or perfect tense (e.g. a gagné).
- For PRESENT activities, look for present tense verbs and words such as maintenant (now) or d'habitude (usually).
- For FUTURE activities, you might find the near future tense (je vais + infinitive) or the future tense (je ferai).

Be careful! The activity in the sentence may be mentioned in the text but make sure it's referred to in the **correct** tense. Here, training twice a week is mentioned in the text but Paul says **Je m'entraînais deux fois par semaine**. (I **used to train** twice a week.)

Now try this · READING · target **C**

Read the text again. Write **T** (true), **F** (false) or **?** (not in the text) for the following sentences.

(a) Paul used to play against another club at the weekends. ☐

(b) His team never won the championship. ☐

(c) He does a martial art. ☐

(d) He plans to take up judo on Thursday evenings. ☐

(e) He has never been water skiing before. ☐

(f) He's been skiing once already. ☐

Going out

Learning vocabulary is essential in preparing for your listening exam. Use the learning tips below.

Sortir

Tu veux sortir?	Do you want to go out?
Tu viens / Vous venez?	Are you coming?
Tu veux / Vous voulez …?	Do you want to …?
aller au cinéma	go to the cinema
aller à la piscine	go to the pool
aller au centre de sport	go to the sports centre
faire du bowling	go bowling
faire une promenade	go for a walk
Je peux / Je ne peux pas …	I can / can't …
Je dois / Il me faut …	I have to …
promener le chien	walk the dog
garder mon petit frère	look after my little brother
faire mes devoirs	do my homework
ranger ma chambre	tidy my room
me relaxer	chill out

tu or vous

FAMILIAR

tu

Use tu (you) to another young person, family member / friend, animal

Use vous (you) to more than one of these people

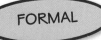

FORMAL

vous

Use vous (you) to adult(s), teacher(s), official(s)

Avoid tu or vous by using on:

On va au stade?

Shall we go to the stadium?

Worked example

 LISTENING 12   target E

Listen to the conversation and complete the two sentences **in English**.

Léa is invited to the …   cinema

She can't go as she has to …   tidy her room

– Salut, Léa! On va au cinéma ce soir. Tu veux venir?

– Oh non, je ne peux pas. Je dois ranger ma chambre!

Learning vocabulary

To prepare for your listening exam, you need to learn lots of vocabulary.

• LOOK at and learn the words.
• COVER the English words.
• WRITE the English words.
• LOOK at all the words.
• SEE how many you have got right.

For an extra challenge, cover the **French** words and repeat the stages above.

Now try this

 LISTENING 13   target E

Listen to the whole recording and complete the sentences with the words or phrases in the box.

(a) Thomas is invited to go to …
(b) He can't go as he has to …
(c) Sarah is invited to go to …
(d) She can't go as she has to …

the leisure centre	the restaurant	the swimming pool
do homework	look after someone	walk the dog

Last weekend

Use the phrases on this page to talk about what you did last weekend.

Le weekend dernier

Je suis allé(e) ...	I went ...
Je suis sorti(e).	I went out.
J'ai regardé (un match).	I watched (a match).
On est parti(e)s.	We left.
J'ai fait la grasse matinée.	I slept in / had a lie-in.
Nous avons vu un film.	We saw a film.
Je suis allé(e) en ville.	I went to town.
J'ai raté le bus.	I missed the bus.
Je me suis levé(e) à dix heures.	I got up at ten o'clock.
On s'est bien amusé(e)s.	We had a good time.
Je me suis cassé la jambe.	I broke my leg.
C'était marrant / génial.	It was funny / great.
Il faisait froid / chaud.	It was cold / hot.
Il y avait du monde.	There were a lot of people.

Irregular past participles

Grammar page 101-102

J'ai ...

bu	drank	pris	took
fait	did	reçu	received
écrit	wrote	vu	saw
lu	read		

See page 45 for verbs which take être in the perfect tense.

On a fait du VTT.

Worked example   READING   target C

Read the text.

> Comme on n'avait pas de cours vendredi dernier, nous avons décidé de faire du VTT. Il faisait beau et chaud, et on est partis avec un piquenique pour aller se baigner au lac. Malheureusement, en rentrant, j'ai eu un accident. Je suis tombée et je me suis cassé la jambe, donc j'ai passé le weekend au lit! Cependant, ce n'était pas du tout ennuyeux car mes copains sont venus chez moi et ont apporté un nouveau DVD. On a passé l'après-midi en regardant un film comique et en mangeant de la pizza!

Answer this question **in English**.

Why did Zoë decide to go mountain biking?

She didn't have lessons on Friday.

Reading tips

- ALWAYS read the WHOLE text through first and get the sense of what happened. THEN look at the questions: do you need to understand every word in the text to answer them?
- Some questions at Grade C will use the PERFECT tense so make sure you are familiar with it – all forms, not just the je form. Check the meaning of the following:

  on est partis   mes copains sont venus
  je suis tombée   ils ont apporté

This question tells you what **VTT** means: mountain biking. It's up to you to work out the meaning of the other words nearby: **Comme on n'avait pas de cours ...** (As we didn't have lessons ...).

Now try this   READING   target C

Read the text again and complete the activity.

(a) What was the weather like?

(b) Name **two** things they were planning to do at the lake.

(c) Why did Zoë end up in bed?

(d) What did Zoë think about being in bed? Why?

Remember that if a question asks for **two details** (like question b) or is in **two parts** (like question d), there are usually **two** marks available.

Television

You need to be able to describe the TYPES of programmes you watch. Don't just give the names of the programmes in English.

La télévision

les actualités / informations (fpl) the news | une comédie de situation a sitcom | un dessin animé a cartoon

un documentaire a documentary | un feuilleton a soap | un jeu télévisé a game show

la météo the weather forcast | la publicité the adverts | une série a series

Pronouncing préféré(e)

Préféré(e) is one of the worst pronounced words by students in the speaking assessment! Pull your lips into a smile and keep them there as you say all three syllables.

une émission
a programme

mon émission préférée
my favourite programme

Une de mes émissions préférées, c'est …
One of my favourite programmes is …

chaîne (de télévision) (f) — television channel
lecteur DVD (m) — DVD player
télévision satellite (f) — satellite television
téléspectateur (m) — TV viewer
sous-titré(e) — subtitled
enregistrer — to record

Worked example

Qu'est-ce que tu aimes regarder à la télé?

Je n'aime pas tellement les jeux télévisés alors je n'en regarde jamais. Je déteste la publicité parce que c'est toujours trop long.

This makes good use of the **adverb tellement** (much) and the **connective alors** (so). The **negative** is accurate and the student **justifies** the reason for disliking adverts using **parce que**.

AIMING HIGHER Je regarde les émissions amusantes et j'adore prendre mon petit déjeuner en regardant ma chaîne préférée. Récemment, j'ai regardé un super bon film qui s'appelle "L'homme, c'est elle", un film américain. Il s'agit d'une fille qui rêve de devenir footballeuse professionnelle. C'est l'un des films les plus drôles que j'ai vu au Festival de Cannes.

This answer is more interesting as it uses plenty of **adjectives** (amusantes, drôles). It also uses the **perfect** tense (j'ai regardé un super bon film) and gives the film title in French, which avoids using English.

Now try this

Prepare answers to these questions. Speak for one minute.
- Quelle est ton émission préférée?
- Pourquoi regardes-tu la télévision?
- Qu'est-ce que tu as regardé récemment?

Cinema

Describing the last film you have seen is a useful topic for a speaking or writing assessment.

Le cinéma

acteur (m) / actrice (f)	actor
film d'aventures (m)	adventure film
film comique (m)	comedy
film de guerre (m)	war film
film d'horreur (m)	horror film
film romantique / d'amour (m)	romance
film de science-fiction (m)	sci-fi film
commencement du film (m)	beginning of the film
écran (m)	screen
effets spéciaux (mpl)	special effects
réduction (f)	reduction
séance (f)	showing
vedette (f)	film star
version originale (VO) (f)	original version
choisir	to choose

avoir expressions

avoir faim / soif	to be hungry / thirsty
avoir raison / tort	to be right / wrong
avoir besoin de	to need
avoir peur	to be afraid
avoir l'air ...	to look ... (angry / sad, etc.)
avoir lieu	to take place
avoir envie (de)	to feel like (doing something)

J'ai peur des films d'horreur. I am afraid of horror films.

Worked example LISTENING 14 target A

Farid and Nathalie are discussing going to the cinema. Which of the following sentences is correct?

A They both want to see the war film.
B They don't agree on what sort of film they want to see.

☐ B

– Regarde, Nathalie – au Gaumont, il y a un film de guerre avec mon acteur préféré. Tu as envie d'y aller voir?

– Non, pas tellement. Ça ne m'intéresse pas.

EXAM ALERT!

This is a higher level listening task, which many students find tricky. Read through the options first and then you will be better prepared for what you're about to hear. Read the instructions **carefully**.

Students have struggled with exam questions similar to this - **be prepared!**

War film (**film de guerre**) is mentioned but Nathalie says Ça ne m'intéresse pas (I'm not interested in it). So although Farid likes it, they don't **both** like it.

Now try this LISTENING 15 target A

Listen to the whole recording and note the **three** correct statements from the list below.

A An English film is showing at the Rex.
B A relative recommended one film.
C Only one film is showing at the Rex.
D The romance starts at 8.30 p.m.
E They decide to see the later film.
F They decide to see the romance.

Don't write more than **three** letters.

☐ ☐ ☐

Music

When writing or talking about music, include your opinion and some personal recollections, to make your text more interesting.

La musique

Mon chanteur préféré / Ma chanteuse préférée, c'est …
My favourite singer is …

J'écoute …	I listen to …
Je suis fan de …	I'm a fan of …
la musique pop / rock	pop / rock
la musique rap / jazz	rap / jazz
la musique classique	classical music
Je joue du piano / de la guitare.	I play the piano / guitar.
chanson (f)	song
groupe (m)	group, band
musicien (m) / musicienne (f)	musician
orchestre (m)	orchestra
tournée (f)	tour
chanter	to sing
écouter la radio	to listen to the radio
télécharger	to download

'this' and 'that' Grammar page 90

THIS / THESE
ce chanteur-ci this singer (male)
cette musicienne-ci this musician (female)
ces mélodies-ci these tunes
THAT / THOSE
ce soir-là that evening
cette tournée-là that tour
ces chansons-là those songs

Ed Sheeran, c'est mon chanteur préféré.

Worked example

Write about your favourite singer.

L'été dernier, avec mes amis, je suis allée voir Rihanna en concert. C'était fantastique et nous avons chanté et dansé pendant tout le concert. Elle était formidable sur scène et je n'oublierai jamais cette soirée-là.

AIMING HIGHER Beyoncé est vraiment une de mes chanteuses préférées et ce serait mon rêve d'aller la voir en concert. D'origine américaine et née à Houston au Texas, elle est considérée comme la personne la plus influente dans le monde de la musique de la décennie 2000–2010. Son premier album solo Dangerously in Love est sorti en 2003. Il a été un des albums les plus vendus de l'année.

This student uses more than one tense: the **perfect** (e.g. je suis allée – I went), the **imperfect** (e.g. c'était – it was) and the **future** (je n'oublierai jamais – I will never forget).

- The **conditional** phrase ce serait mon rêve de + infinitive (it would be my dream to) is useful in lots of topics.
- Note also the good command of **superlatives**: la personne la plus influente (the most influential person) and un des albums les plus vendus (one of the highest-selling albums).

Now try this

Write about your favourite music group or solo artist. Write 100–150 words.

- Explain why you have chosen this person.
- Give some background details on him / her.
- List his / her key successes.

- Describe an occasion when you saw him / her live, or express your hopes to do so in the future.

New technology

This page will help you talk about some online activities if you are preparing a text about your hobbies.

La technologie

mon ordinateur	my computer
Je tchate.	I talk online.
Je joue à des jeux.	I play games.
Je visite des forums.	I visit chatrooms.

Je surfe sur Internet.
I surf the internet.

Je vais sur mon site perso.
I go to my own site.

Je cherche des informations.
I look for information.

J'envoie des e-mails.   I send emails.

Je reçois du courrier électronique.
I receive emails.

Je mets des photos en ligne.
I upload photos.

Je regarde des émissions de télé.
I watch TV programmes.

Je sauvegarde de la musique.
I store music.

Je télécharge de la musique.
I download music.

mon portable
my mobile

J'envoie des textos.
I send texts.

Je reçois des textos.
I receive texts.

Je bavarde avec mes amis.
I chat to my friends.

Je prends des photos.
I take photos.

Present tense: irregular verbs

envoyer	to send	➡	j'envoie	I send
aller	to go	➡	je vais	I go
mettre en ligne	to upload	➡	je mets en ligne	I upload
s'appeler	to be called	➡	je m'appelle	I am called
se lever	to get up	➡	je me lève	I get up
recevoir	to receive	➡	je reçois	I receive

Worked example

What does this person use new technology for? Complete the sentence.

This girl ... chats with her friends ... on her mobile.

– J'ai un portable et je bavarde avec mes amis.

Listening strategies

- Before you listen, LOOK through the vocabulary above on new technology and think about what you may hear.
- This type of activity is all about listening for KEY WORDS – there are no opinions, alternatives or negatives.
- Rather than leave a blank, write something sensible even if you don't understand everything.

Now try this

Listen to four more people and note what they use the internet for. Complete the sentences.

1 This boy ... every day.
2 This girl ... on her computer.
3 This boy ...
4 This girl ... with her mobile.

Internet language

Some technical internet language is listed below. Try to use comparatives wherever you can.

La langue d'Internet

l'écran (tactile) (m) (touch) screen

le clavier keyboard

la touche key

l'ordinateur (m) computer

l'imprimante (f) printer

la souris mouse

e-mail / courrier électronique (m)	email
fichier (m)	file
logiciel (m)	software
mot de passe (m)	password
page d'accueil (f)	welcome page
site Internet / web (m)	website
traitement de texte (m)	word processing
cliquer	to click
effacer	to delete
mettre en ligne	to upload
sauvegarder	to save
taper	to type
télécharger	to download
numérique	digital

Comparatives

> Grammar page 89

Put plus (more) / moins (less) / aussi (as) + que around an adjective to compare things.

La souris est plus vieille que l'ordinateur.
The mouse is older than the computer.

Mon ordinateur était moins cher que le tien.
My computer was less expensive than yours.

Je tape aussi vite que toi.
I type as quickly as you.

Worked example

Read this extract from a text.

> Nous avons sélectionné pour vous la meilleure solution pour sauvegarder vos fichiers et les protéger contre les virus, grâce à un logiciel aussi simple qu'efficace ... et en plus, c'est gratuit.

Answer the question **in English**.

(a) What **two** things does this software claim to do? save your files, protect them from viruses

Aiming higher

You need to read for DETAIL in order to give precise answers. Reading for gist alone will not be enough to answer the questions correctly.

Knowledge of vocabulary is vital in this type of task: **sauvegarder vos fichiers** (save your files) and **les protéger contre les virus** (protect them from viruses).

The question asks for **two** claims, not just one: make sure you read the question carefully and answer it completely.

Now try this

Read the text again and complete the activity.

(b) Give **two** of the software's attributes.

Don't ignore the final adjective gratuit – use this if you are struggling to understand the others listed, but do not list all **three** as you risk introducing errors.

Internet pros and cons

Try to memorise a few phrases on this page to talk about internet pros and cons.

Positif et négatif d'Internet

avantage (m)   advantage

désavantage / inconvénient (m)   disadvantage

Internet, c'est un moyen pratique de ...

The internet is a good way of ...

   s'informer.

   keeping up-to-date.

   acheter des billets de train / cinéma.

   buying train / cinema tickets.

   rester en contact avec ses amis.

   keeping in touch with friends.

   jouer à des jeux.

   playing games.

Internet, c'est dangereux / mauvais quand on ...

The internet is dangerous when you ...

   ne surveille pas les enfants.

   don't keep an eye on children.

   passe tout son temps libre devant l'écran.

   spend all your free time in front of the screen.

   donne ses coordonnées sur un forum.

   give your details in a chatroom.

Opinion phrases

Add an opinion phrase wherever possible to personalise your work.

À mon avis, les parents doivent savoir avec qui leurs enfants communiquent en ligne.
In my opinion, parents should know who their children are communicating with online.

Selon moi, on ne doit pas rester en ligne après huit heures du soir.
I feel you shouldn't stay online after 8 p.m.

Personnellement, je trouve que sur Internet, les livres coûtent moins cher.
Personally, I find that books cost less on the internet.

Les problèmes les plus graves, ce sont les inconvénients techniques.
The biggest problems are technical hitches.

 Je fais des recherches pour mes devoirs.

 Je fais des achats en ligne.

Worked example SPEAKING

Tu aimes utiliser Internet?

J'utilise Internet pour faire des recherches pour mes devoirs, pour faire des achats, pour contacter mes amis ... pour tout.

This response is unlikely to achieve a high grade because it does not give an **opinion**, there is only one **tense** and it simply lists activities.

AIMING HIGHER Selon moi, Internet est un moyen rapide d'accéder à toute l'information, mais on ne doit pas oublier les inconvénients. Personnellement, je pense que le problème le plus grave, c'est qu'il y a des gens qui harcèlent les autres en ligne. La semaine dernière, on a piraté l'ordinateur de mon frère et un inconnu a fait des achats avec sa carte de crédit. Il dit qu'il ne fera plus d'achats en ligne.

CONTROLLED ASSESSMENT

To give the best answer, try to use a wide range of appropriate and interesting vocabulary, together with a variety of structures, including some complex items. You should also aim to express and explain a range of ideas and points of view.

Il y a des gens qui harcèlent ... = There are people who harass ...

Now try this SPEAKING

Speak for 30–40 seconds about the following: • Parle des avantages et des inconvénients d'Internet.

Shops

Make sure you learn the names of shops. Notice that all those ending in -ie are feminine.

Les magasins

 la bijouterie   la boucherie   la boulangerie

 la charcuterie   la chocolaterie   la confiserie

 le fleuriste   la librairie   la pâtisserie

 la pharmacie   la poissonnerie   le supermarché

Present tense -er verbs

 Grammar page 95

Use the present tense to talk about what you are doing NOW or do REGULARLY.

je joue	I play
tu joues	you play
il / elle / on joue	he / she / one plays
nous jouons	we play
vous jouez	you play
ils / elles jouent	they play

Aimes-tu ce magasin?
Do you like this shop?

Nous achetons du poisson.
We buy / are buying fish.

Notice the je, tu, il / elle and ils / elles forms:

acheter   to buy   ➡   j'achète   I buy

préférer   to prefer ➡ elle préfère   she prefers

Worked example

READING   target **G**

Read the sign on this shop.

What does this shop sell?   perfume

 Read the sign carefully — it is the sort of cognate you should easily recognise.

Learning vocabulary

In the reading and listening exams you need to RECOGNISE French words, not PRODUCE them, so when you are revising vocabulary for these exams, concentrate on testing yourself on FRENCH TO ENGLISH, rather than the other way round.

jouer = to play, so you should be able to work out what jouets means.

Now try this

READING   target **G**

What shops are these? Write the correct letter in each box.

1 un magasin de sport ☐   4 un magasin de musique ☐   **A** toy shop   **D** furniture shop

2 un magasin de bricolage ☐   5 un magasin de jouets ☐   **B** music shop   **E** sports shop

3 un magasin de meubles ☐   **C** DIY shop

Food shopping

Quantities are useful expressions to know when shopping in France.

Faire les courses

un kilo de	a kilo of
un litre de	a litre of
un morceau de	a piece of
un paquet de	a packet of
un peu de	a little of / a few
une moitié de	a half of
une boîte de	a box of
une bouteille de	a bottle of
une douzaine de	a dozen
une tranche de	a slice of
champignon (m)	mushroom
chou (m)	cabbage
fraise (f)	strawberry
pomme (f)	apple
œuf (m)	egg
pêche (f)	peach
pomme de terre (f)	potato
raisins (mpl)	grapes
yaourt (m)	yoghurt

Quantities

After quantities, de does not change to agree with the noun. It stays as de. Before a vowel, it becomes d'.

assez de	enough
beaucoup de	lots of
encore de	more
moins de	less
pas mal de	quite a few
plein de	a lot of
plus de	more

Elle a assez de bananes.
She's got enough bananas.

Tu as trop d'argent.
You have got too much money.

Il y a plein de pommes.
There are plenty of apples.

Worked example

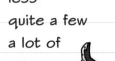

Listen to this dialogue in a shop and answer the question **in English**.

How much water is needed?   2 bottles

> – Bonjour, monsieur. Je voudrais une bouteille d'eau minérale, s'il vous plaît.
> – Une bouteille d'...
> – Non, pardon, nous avons besoin de deux bouteilles.
> – Pas de problème – voilà deux bouteilles d'eau.

nous avons besoin de = we need

Listening strategies

- Don't be too HASTY to write down your answers – requests sometimes change, so you need to listen until the end!
- If you do change your mind about an answer, make sure you cross it out completely and write the correct answer clearly instead.
- When speaking normally, especially in dialogues, people often use 'thinking' noises: don't be put off by them! You can use your own 'thinking' noises to gain time in your speaking assessment.
  Euh ... Er ...   Ah ... Er ...
  Attends / Attendez ... Er, wait ...

Now try this

Listen to the rest of the dialogue. Fill in the missing quantities or items **in English**.

(a) ... of biscuits
(b) one kilo of ...
(c) ... of ham

(d) ... of mushrooms
(e) a dozen ...
(f) ... of chocolate cake

Shopping

You may need to describe items you would like to buy – remember to make adjectives agree.

Faire des achats

des bijoux (mpl)

un bonnet

une casquette

une ceinture

un chapeau

le maquillage

le rouge à lèvres

un sac à dos

le parfum

achats (mpl)	purchases
cadeau (m)	present
caisse (f)	till
rayon (m)	department
soldes (mpl)	sales

efficace	efficient
fonctionner	to work

Using the adjective 'new'

nouveau (new) = irregular adjective

singular		plural	
masc	fem	masc	fem
nouveau	nouvelle	nouveaux	nouvelles

Use **nouvel** in front of a masculine singular noun starting with a vowel or silent h.

un **nouvel** accessoire   a new accessory

une **nouvelle** bague   a new ring

When 'new' means 'different' (e.g. if you want a new glass to replace a dirty one) use **autre** (other):

Est-ce que je peux avoir un autre verre?
Can I have a new (another) glass?

Read the text.

Le bonnet MP3
C'est le nouvel accessoire indispensable pour les jeunes, les fanatiques de la mode et de la bonne musique. Vous pouvez tout simplement relier votre lecteur MP3 au récepteur fourni dans votre bonnet. Puis mettez le récepteur dans votre poche ou votre sac et écoutez vos chansons favorites – sans fil. La transmission du récepteur au bonnet est efficace jusqu'à 12 mètres. L'émetteur ainsi que le récepteur fonctionnent chacun avec deux piles AAA (non incluses).

Answer this question **in English**.

Name two types of people who might buy this product. *young people, music fans*

Reading strategies

In questions aimed at higher grades, there may be some vocabulary you won't know. Here are some strategies:

- READ the English questions to find out more information.

- Recognising COGNATES will help: indispensable, fanatique, musique, accessoire. But be careful: piles are batteries, not piles!

- Use CONTEXT – the text is about an MP3 player and earphones, so the chances are that un récepteur is some sort of receiver (it isn't crucial to know which sort exactly).

Read the text again and answer the questions **in English**.

(a) What do you have to do to make the device work?
(b) Which **two** places are suggested for placing the receiver?
(c) How close must the receiver be to the earphones?

Clothes

Trousers, jeans, pyjamas and shorts are plural in English but in French they are all singular.

Les vêtements

 des baskets

 une chemise

 un chemisier

 un jean

 une jupe

 un pantalon

 un pull(-over)

 un pyjama

une robe

 des sandales

 un short

un sweat

Position of adjectives   Grammar page 87

All colours (les couleurs) and most other adjectives come AFTER the noun:
la robe bleue = the blue dress.

- rouge
- gris(e)
- jaune
- noir(e)
- marron

- bleu(e)
- vert(e)
- blanc / blanche
- rose

The adjectives **marron** and **rose** do not change in the feminine or plural: **une chemise marron, deux chemises marron.**

rayé(e)	striped
en coton / en soie	cotton / silk
en laine	woollen
(bleu) clair / foncé	light / dark (blue)

Worked example LISTENING 20   target D

Listen and answer this question.
What did this person buy and why? F 2

Make sure you read the question carefully. Here you have to note **two** pieces of information.

 A

 B

 C

If there are pictures to choose from, try to go through them **before** you listen and remind yourself of the French for each item.

 D

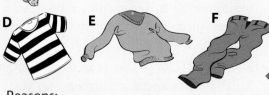 E

F

EXAM ALERT!

Make sure you know how cognates are pronounced. They may look similar to English words, but they sound quite different. Knowledge of core vocab is vital in both reading **and** listening.

Students have struggled with exam questions similar to this - **be prepared!**

Reasons:

1 the material	2 the colour	3 holidays
4 the price	5 the size	6 the shop

– J'ai acheté ce pantalon parce que j'aime la couleur.

Now try this LISTENING 21   target D

Listen to the rest of the recording. What item did these people buy and why? Write the letter of the item and the number of the reason from the lists above.

1 ☐ ☐   2 ☐ ☐   3 ☐ ☐   4 ☐ ☐

Clothes shopping

If you are talking about clothes shopping in your speaking assessment, make sure you are familiar with ways of asking questions.

Faire du shopping

un blouson

des bottes

une cravate

une écharpe

des gants

un imper(méable)

un maillot de bain

un manteau

un pull à capuche

acheter	to buy		
boutique (f)	small shop	à la mode	fashionable
marque (f)	brand / make / label	démodé(e)	old-fashioned
taille (f)	size	ridicule	ridiculous

Asking questions

Grammar page 108

1 Raise your voice to turn a statement into a question.

Vous aimez acheter des vêtements?
Do you like buying clothes?

2 Put Est-ce que at the start of a question.

Est-ce que vous aimez acheter des vêtements?
Do you like buying clothes?

3 Swap the subject and verb round and add a hyphen.

Aimez-vous acheter des vêtements?
Do you like buying clothes?

Add a -t- between two vowels:

Ton frère, aime-t-il faire du shopping?
Does your brother like going shopping?

Worked example

SPEAKING

Tu aimes faire du shopping?

Je n'aime pas trop acheter des vêtements parce que je trouve cela ennuyeux. J'ai mon propre style et je trouve la mode complètement ridicule. Je préfère acheter des magazines ou des livres.

* Good use of **ne ... trop** (not much) makes a change from just **ne ... pas**.
* Use **parce que** ... to **justify** an opinion.

AIMING HIGHER

J'aime m'habiller à la mode et chaque weekend je vais en ville pour faire du shopping. De temps en temps, on peut trouver des marques à de super prix. La semaine dernière, j'ai acheté un T-shirt dans une liquidation de stock. J'étais très heureuse et ce samedi, je voudrais retourner au centre-ville chercher des bottes et un blouson!

* **Variety** of structures, tenses, interesting vocabulary and opinions all help aim for a higher grade.
* The use of **present**, **perfect** (things bought last week) and **conditional** (je voudrais retourner – I'd like to return) also helps to raise the level.

Now try this

SPEAKING

Answer these questions. Say at least 2–3 sentences in reply to each.

* Pour toi, c'est important d'être à la mode?
* Aimes-tu faire du shopping?
* Est-ce que tu achètes souvent des marques? Pourquoi (pas)?

Pocket money

Make sure you can talk about pocket money and can use possessive adjectives correctly.

L'argent de poche

Je dépense …	I spend …
Je fais des économies.	I save.
J'achète des cadeaux.	I buy presents.
Je gagne dix livres sterling.	I earn ten pounds.
Je mets de l'argent à côté.	I put money aside.
Je reçois …	I receive …
Mes parents me donnent …	My parents give me …
Mes parents ne me donnent pas d'argent.	My parents don't give me money.
Ils paient (mes vêtements).	They pay for (my clothes).
Avec mon argent, j'achète …	With my money I buy …
Je trouve ça injuste.	I find that unfair.
Je trouve ça généreux.	I find that generous.
Je dois aider à la maison.	I have to help at home.

Possessive adjectives

	masc	fem	plural
my	mon	ma	mes
your	ton	ta	tes
his / her	son	sa	ses
our	notre		nos
your	votre		vos
their	leur		leurs

Je lave leur voiture.
I wash their car.

Worked example 22 target B

Listen to Clément. Write the letters for the **two** things he mentions.

Ⓐ Ⓖ

A	I look after a relative.
B	I think what I get is unfair.
C	I buy presents.
D	I think what I get is very generous.
E	I help with the housework.
F	My parents buy my clothes.
G	I am saving to buy something I like.
H	I have no money to buy computer games.

– Clément, tes parents te donnent de l'argent?
– Oui, ils me donnent 60 euros par mois mais je dois les gagner! Je lave leur voiture et je dois garder ma petite sœur quand mes parents sortent. Je trouve ça assez généreux. J'essaie de faire des économies puis je peux acheter des jeux électroniques de temps en temps.

Listening tips

In this type of question, look through all the options carefully BEFORE you listen and try to PREDICT what language you are likely to hear.

- Clément says **Je dois garder ma petite sœur**. The options do not mention **sœur** but they **do** mention looking after a relative, so A must be correct.
- Clément also says **J'essaie de faire des économies**. If you have looked at the vocab list above, you will know that this means save money – so G must be correct.
- He also says **Je trouve ça assez généreux** so you may think that D is correct – but be careful of small words: **assez** means 'quite', not 'very', so D is not correct.

Now try this 23 target B

Now listen to Amélie and Raoul and note **two** things each of them mentions from the list above. Write the correct letters in the boxes.

1 Amélie ☐ ☐   **2** Raoul ☐ ☐

Had a look ☐   Nearly there ☐   Nailed it! ☐

Holiday destinations

Use this page to talk accurately about where you go on holiday.

Où on va en vacances

Je passe mes vacances ...	I spend my holidays ...
Je vais en Espagne.	I go to Spain.
Je suis allé(e) ...	I went ...
en Allemagne	to Germany
en Amérique	to America
en Australie / Chine	to Australia / China
en Suisse	to Switzerland
en Tunisie	to Tunisia
en Afrique / Belgique	to Africa / Belgium
en Inde	to India
au Canada / Japon	to Canada / Japan
au Portugal	to Portugal
à l'étranger	abroad
dans une station balnéaire	to a beach resort
à la côte	to the coast
au bord de la mer	to / at the seaside
à la campagne	to / in the countryside
à la montagne	to / in the mountains
dans un village	to / in a village

How to say 'to'

masc	fem	starting with vowel	plural
au	à la	à l'	aux

J'adore passer les vacances au bord de la mer.
I love spending the holidays by the sea.

Je suis allé à l'étranger. I went abroad.

J'aime passer les vacances à la campagne.
I like holidaying in the countryside.

à + town
à Paris = to / in Paris
en or au + most countries
en Angleterre = to / in England

Worked example

 READING   target B

Read the text.

Je m'appelle Célia et cette année je vais passer les vacances chez mes grands-parents qui habitent un village à la campagne, parce que mes parents travaillent. Ma copine Murielle va aller avec toute sa famille au camping la Forêt, au Lavandou. C'est une station balnéaire dans le Midi près de St Tropez.
Le père de mon cousin Rayan insiste toujours pour aller à la montagne, où il doit faire beaucoup de randonnées ou de VTT.

Who is going to stay with relatives?
Write **C** (for Célia), **M** (for Murielle) or **R** (for Rayan). ☐ C

EXAM ALERT!

This tests the ability to read a short text and identify which characters in it do particular things. It involves deductive reasoning and knowledge of a varied vocabulary. In this sort of activity, the questions don't necessarily follow the order of the text.

Students have struggled with exam questions similar to this - **be prepared!**

You have **three** names to choose from and each one of them has relatives who are connected in some way with their holiday plans – **père, famille, grands-parents, cousin** – but only **one** person is actually staying with relatives: look for **chez**.

Now try this

 READING   target B

Read the text again. Write **C** (for Célia), **M** (for Murielle) or **R** (for Rayan).

(a) Who does not go on holiday with their parents? ☐

(b) Who is going on a seaside holiday? ☐

(c) Who will do mountain biking? ☐

(d) Who will spend their holiday in a tent? ☐

(e) Whose parents don't go on holiday? ☐

Holiday accommodation

Use different tenses when talking about holidays, to aim for a higher grade.

Le logement

loger	to stay
réserver	to book
appartement loué (m)	rented flat
auberge de jeunesse (f)	youth hostel
chambre d'hôte (f)	bed and breakfast
gîte (m)	holiday home
hôtel (m)	hotel
chez des copains	with friends
complet / complète	full
confortable	comfortable
spacieux / spacieuse	spacious

au printemps   en été

en automne   en hiver

Aiming higher

Use tense markers together with a range of tenses to aim for a higher grade:

✓ PRESENT

toujours	always
d'habitude	usually

Cette année on va dans un camping.
We are going to a campsite this year.

✓ PAST

il y a longtemps	a long time ago
l'été dernier	last summer

Avant, on louait un gîte.
Before, we used to rent a holiday home.

✓ FUTURE and NEAR FUTURE

l'année prochaine	next year
dans quelques semaines	in a few weeks' time

À l'avenir, je réserverai une chambre à l'avance.
In future I will reserve a room in advance.

Worked example

Write about your holidays.

D'habitude, on loue un appartement dans une grande résidence avec piscine et salle de jeux, mais l'été dernier, on est restés chez des copains à la montagne et cela a été un désastre.

AIMING HIGHER
Cet été, pour la première fois, je vais rester chez moi. Normalement, je vais en vacances avec ma famille, mais l'année dernière j'ai décidé de ne plus le faire parce que mon petit frère m'énervait trop. Alors j'ai trouvé un petit emploi dans un restaurant où je vais travailler pendant la saison pour gagner de l'argent. À la fin des vacances, j'espère aller chez ma copine en Italie, toute seule!

These sentences hang together well, with an easy progression from the **present** tense (with **d'habitude**) flowing on to the **perfect** tense, introduced very naturally by **mais l'été dernier** (but last summer) + an opinion. A sound piece of writing.

- This text deserves a higher grade as it flows well and uses a **variety of tenses** + tense markers.
- It also uses **interesting structures**: **espérer** + infinitive (to hope to), **pour** + infinitive (in order to) and **toute seule** (all alone) with the correct adjective agreement.

Now try this

Write about 200 words on your holidays. Mention where you:
- usually stay on holiday
- once stayed on holiday
- will stay next holiday
- would like to stay.

Booking accommodation

The verb pouvoir (can) needs an infinitive: je peux aller (I can go).

Réservations

arrivée (f)	arrival
bagages (mpl)	luggage
balcon (m)	balcony
chambre (pour une personne) (f)	single room
chambre pour deux personnes (f)	double room
chambre double (f)	double room
demi-pension (f)	half-board
pension-complète (f)	full board
vue (f)	view
pour trois nuits	for three nights
Bon séjour!	Have a nice stay!
compris / inclus	included

Nous allons arriver vers minuit.
We are going to arrive around midnight.

Il faut réserver en avance.
You have to book in advance.

Using pouvoir

Grammar page 99

PRESENT

je peux	I can
tu peux	you can
il / elle / on peut	he / she / one can
nous pouvons	we can
vous pouvez	you can
ils / elles peuvent	they can

IMPERFECT
je pouvais = I used to be able to

FUTURE
je pourrai = I will be able to

CONDITIONAL je pourrais = I could

Nous pouvons nager dans la mer.

Worked example

LISTENING 24 · target C

Listen and note the correct letter.
Juliette has booked rooms for:
A 2nd–10th April
B 10th–12th April
C 12th–14th April
☐ B

– Quelles sont les dates pour notre weekend à Paris?
– J'ai réservé du dix au douze avril.

Listening tips

In the listening exam, there will always be one or two questions which test numbers. Don't confuse deux = 2, dix = 10 and douze = 12:
du dix au douze avril = from 10th to 12th April.

EXAM ALERT!

When you do Now Try This, listen carefully for negatives to avoid jumping to the wrong conclusion: **ne … plus** = no longer. So **il ne peut plus y aller** = he can no longer go.

Students have struggled with exam questions similar to this - **be prepared!**

Now try this

LISTENING 25 · target C

Listen to the rest of the recording and complete the activity.

1 Tom …
A can no longer go with them
B has to take an exam before he leaves
C wants a double room ☐

2 The rooms …
A have no balcony
B don't have a good view
C have a balcony ☐

3 The reservation made is for …
A breakfast and dinner included
B breakfast, lunch and dinner included
C bed and breakfast ☐

Staying in a hotel

Be prepared to talk about where you stay on holiday – and don't forget negatives!

Loger dans un hôtel

ascenseur (m)	lift
chambre de famille (f)	family room
clef / clé (f)	key
climatisation (f)	air conditioning
avec douche / bain	with shower / bath
entrée (f)	entrance
escalier (m)	staircase
jardin (m)	garden
lavabo (m)	sink
liste des prix (f) / tarif (m)	price list
parking (m)	car park
plage (f)	beach
premier / deuxième étage (m)	first / second floor
réception (f)	reception
rez-de-chaussée (m)	ground floor
salle de bains (f)	bathroom
salle de jeux (f)	games room
vue de la mer (f)	sea view
marcher	to work

Negatives

Grammar page 101

Negatives go either side of the verb, forming a sandwich.

ne + pas = not
ne + plus = no longer
ne + jamais = never
ne + personne = nobody
ne + guère = hardly
ne + que = only
ne + rien = nothing
ne + ni + ni = neither ... nor ...

La climatisation ne marchait pas.
The air conditioning wasn't working.

Note the position with the perfect tense, around the auxiliary verb.

Elle n'a pas choisis un bon hôtel.

Worked example

  READING target A

Read the text.

> Après avoir lu toutes les brochures des hôtels dans le Midi, Lila a choisi un petit hôtel familial qui donnait sur la plage. Il y avait une piscine et une salle de jeux pour les enfants et pour les grands-parents il y avait la climatisation et un ascenseur. Mais, en arrivant, toute la famille a été vraiment déçue. L'hôtel était en construction et la famille ne pouvait ni voir la plage ni dormir la nuit à cause du bruit. Il n'y avait rien à faire pour les enfants et la climatisation ne marchait pas. La famille ne retournera jamais à cet hôtel.

Brochures is a cognate meaning 'brochures', but **après avoir lu** (after having read) is more complicated. Try to learn irregular past participles such as **lu**.

Answer the question **in English**.
How did Lila choose her holiday accommodation?
She read all the brochures.

Make sure you answer **in English**. If you answer in French, it will not be counted.

Now try this

  READING target A

Two details are required for questions b and c, so make sure you write **two** things.

Answer the questions **in English**.

(a) Where did Lila go on holiday?
(b) Name **one** facility for the young and **one** for older people which made the hotel suitable.
(c) Why did the hotel not match the family's expectations? Give **two** details.
(d) What did the family feel about their stay by the end?

Camping

If you have learnt some sentences about camping for your speaking assessment, make sure you can adapt them to answer the questions you're asked!

Au camping

faire du camping	to go camping
aire de jeux (f)	play area
bloc sanitaire (m)	shower block
camping (m)	campsite
caravane (f)	caravan
colonie de vacances (f)	summer camp
eau potable (f)	drinking water
emplacement (m)	pitch (on campsite)
lieu (m)	place
location de vélos (f)	bike hire
parc d'attractions (m)	amusement park
randonnée (f)	hike
sac de couchage (m)	sleeping bag
en plein air	outside
J'attends avec beaucoup d'impatience …	
I'm really looking forward to …	

Alternatives to aller

Try to vary not only the tenses of verbs, but also the verbs themselves.

- arriver — to arrive
- conduire — to drive
- entrer — to enter
- rouler — to go along (in a car)
- marcher — to walk
- **aller — to go**
- venir — to come
- partir — to leave
- visiter — to visit (place)
- passer — to pass by
- quitter — to leave
- rentrer / retourner — to return

Worked example

SPEAKING

Parle de tes vacances.

Chaque année, je retourne au même camping avec ma famille. Le voyage dure trois heures en voiture et le camping se trouve au bord du lac. J'aime bien faire des excursions au parc d'attractions et à la mer, mais ce que je n'aime pas, ce sont les randonnées fatigantes à la montagne.

AIMING HIGHER

Les grandes vacances, c'est le meilleur moment de l'année parce que je quitte la maison pour aller en colonie de vacances. J'adore ça et cet été on va camper en plein air. J'attends mes vacances avec beaucoup d'impatience parce que ça sera une nouvelle expérience pour moi. J'espère qu'il fera beau et qu'il ne pleuvra pas tout le temps!

CONTROLLED ASSESSMENT

To aim for a higher mark, you need to have an accurate accent and intonation. Practise recording yourself and listening back to see how French you sound. Also, when asked questions, you need to respond appropriately and show initiative!

This student restricts herself to the **present tense**, but she gives a **positive** and a **negative** opinion of holiday activities.

This response talks about a specific camping trip in the **future**.

The use of expressions such as **J'espère que** (I hope that) confirms the student's ability to use more **complex language**.

Now try this

SPEAKING

Prepare for a conversation about holidays. You could be asked the following:

- What is your favourite sort of holiday?
- Do you like camping? Why / Why not?
- Describe a school trip you've been on in the past.
- Say what holiday you'd like to have in the future.

Think up **two** more questions you could be asked.

Had a look ☐   Nearly there ☐   Nailed it! ☐

Holiday activities

Be prepared to talk about what you can do on holiday, as well as about where you go.

Activités de vacances

On peut ...   You can ...

se baigner

se bronzer

écrire des cartes postales

faire du canoë kayak

regarder les feux d'artifice

faire du surf

faire de la plongée sous-marine

faire de la planche à voile

jouer au ping-pong

aller à la pêche

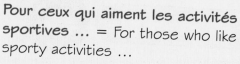

faire des sports nautiques

faire de l'alpinisme

How to say 'this' and 'these'

Grammar page 90

ce	this + masculine nouns
cet	this + masculine nouns starting with a vowel or silent h
cette	this + feminine nouns
ces	these + ALL plural nouns

Cet été je vais en France.
I am going to France this summer.

Cette année je vais me baigner.
This year I'm going to swim.

Pendant ces vacances il va jouer au ping-pong.
During these holidays he is going to play table tennis.

ceux = those
Pour ceux qui aiment les activités sportives ... = For those who like sporty activities ...

Worked example

READING   target C

What does this person say about holidays? Choose the correct sentence ending from A–G.

En été ...   C

A	aller à la pêche.
B	regardez les feux d'artifice.
C	je préfère faire de la planche à voile.
D	fait les sports nautiques tous les jours.
E	vont écrire des cartes postales.
F	vais faire du canoë kayak cette année.
G	allons essayer de la plongée sous-marine.

Gapped activities

You have to know your grammar for this type of activity (e.g. verb endings).

- First of all, make sure you READ through all the options to work out what they mean.
- In the Worked example, what would make sense after En été ...? It can only be C because it's the only one that starts with a PRONOUN.
- In Now Try This, look at number 4: Cet été, nous ... This shows you that you need to look for a VERB in the nous form. What ending are you looking for?

Now try this

READING   target C

Now choose the correct sentence ending from A–G above for these four people. Write the correct letter in each box.

1 Je pense que ... ☐

2 En vacances, mon frère ... ☐

3 Mon père adore ... ☐

4 Cet été, nous ... ☐

Holiday preferences

This page will help you give opinions about holidays in lots of different ways.

Les vacances que j'aime

C'est / C'était ...	It is / It was ...
chouette / génial	great
fantastique / formidable	brilliant
intéressant / ennuyeux	interesting / boring
Ce n'est pas mon truc.	It's not my thing.

Ce que j'aime, c'est me bronzer.
What I like is sunbathing.

Le plus important, c'est de faire du sport.
The most important thing is to do sport.

Quand j'étais petit(e), ça allait.
When I was young it was OK.

J'adore être en plein air, même quand il pleut.
I love being outdoors even when it rains.

Ce que j'aime le plus, c'est aller à la piscine.
What I like the most is going to the pool.

Expressing likes and dislikes

adorer	to love
aimer	to like
préférer	to prefer — + infinitive
je n'aime pas	I dislike
détester	to hate

J'adore faire du camping.
I love camping.

Je préfère loger dans un hôtel.
I prefer staying in a hotel.

Worked example

WRITING

Write about holidays you don't like!

> L'été dernier, je suis allée à Londres, mais je n'ai pas du tout aimé. Je déteste visiter des monuments et des sites historiques parce que ce n'est pas mon truc. Ce que j'aime faire, c'est aller à la piscine et me bronzer toute la journée avec mes copains.

AIMING HIGHER

> D'habitude, nous restons dans un grand gîte au bord de la mer, mais cette année on va passer des vacances à la campagne parce qu'il faut économiser. Nous allons faire du camping et ce n'est pas mon truc! Mon père a trouvé un petit camping pas cher dans une forêt, mais je préférerais aller à la plage parce que j'adore nager et me bronzer.

Aiming higher

To aim for a higher grade, you must link your sentences into a coherent whole. Even linking sentences with a simple conjunction such as mais (but) will help your work flow.

This answer starts off by mentioning a **past** holiday and **opinion** in the past, and then switches to the **present** tense and expresses a preference.

- This version uses lots of tenses including **present**, **perfect** and **future**, as well as the **conditional**.
- **Different** parts of verbs are used: I, he and we.
- Correct **adjective agreements** are indicators of a top level response.

Now try this

WRITING

Write about your holiday preferences. Include information about:
- what you usually do
- what you are doing this year
- your opinion.

Read through your text **carefully** – does it hang together well?

Holiday plans

Make sure you know the future tense in order to talk about holiday plans. Ring the changes by using the nous form (we) as well as je.

Projets de vacances

pendant les grandes vacances
in the summer holiday(s)

vacances de neige (fpl)
winter sports holiday

l'été / l'hiver prochain (m)
next summer / winter

demain	tomorrow
après-demain	the day after tomorrow
le lendemain	the next day
louer	to rent
port de pêche (m)	fishing port
J'irai …	I will go …
On mangera …	We will eat …

Nous passerons la journée …
We will spend the day …

The nous form in the future tense

NEAR FUTURE

Nous allons voyager en Afrique.
We are going to travel across Africa.

FUTURE TENSE

Nous irons en Autriche.
We will go to Austria.

Nous aurons une chambre dans un hôtel.
We will have a room in a hotel.

Nous ferons de la planche à voile.
We will do windsurfing.

Worked example

Write about your holiday plans for this year.

Pendant les grandes vacances, j'irai au Lavandou avec ma famille. Nous allons louer un appartement dans une grande résidence avec piscine à cinq-cents mètres de la plage. On y va depuis huit ans!

AIMING HIGHER Voulez-vous passer des vacances avec moi? L'été prochain, nous irons à une station balnéaire qui s'appelle La Baule, où il y a une des plus belles plages d'Europe. Vous pouvez y trouver cinquante plages, six ports de pêche et de plaisance et plus de cent courts de tennis. Vous pourriez jouer au golf sur un des deux terrains de golf à 18 et 9 trous.

Aiming higher

In your writing tasks, remember to use different tenses, descriptions and opinions as well as more complex language to achieve the best written work.

✓ For added VARIETY, swap between the nous form (nous allons) and the on form (on va – same ending as 3rd person singular).

✓ Add a RHETORICAL QUESTION to the reader, such as Voulez-vous passer des vacances avec moi?

✓ Include DIFFERENT STRUCTURES in your writing, such as depuis + present tense, as well as the future tense with nous and je.

Now try this

Write about your future holiday plans in about 100 words.

Try to include:
- several forms of verbs (vous, je, nous, on)
- several tenses (future, present)
- comparatives (plus de) and superlatives (une des plus belles plages d'Europe)
- relative pronouns (une station balnéaire qui s'appelle …).

Holiday experiences

'Past holidays' is a popular topic for reading exams. Make sure you learn winter holiday vocabulary too, as France is a big skiing country.

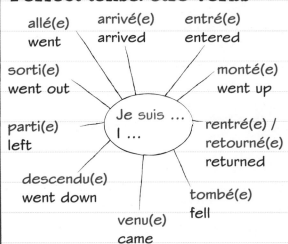

Grammar page 102

Les vacances de l'année dernière

dortoir (m)	dormitory
logement (m)	accommodation
nourriture (f)	food
stage de ski (m)	skiing course
vacances d'hiver (fpl)	winter holidays
valises (fpl)	suitcases
en hiver	in winter
j'ai fait	I did
j'ai vu	I saw
nous sommes sorti(e)s	we went out
nous avons partagé	we shared
c'était	it was
Ce n'était pas mal.	It wasn't bad.
Les vacances étaient …	The holidays were …

J'ai fait du snowboard.

Perfect tense: être verbs

allé(e) — went
arrivé(e) — arrived
entré(e) — entered
sorti(e) — went out
monté(e) — went up
parti(e) — left
rentré(e) / retourné(e) — returned
descendu(e) — went down
tombé(e) — fell
venu(e) — came

Je suis … / I …

The past participle has to AGREE with the subject:

je suis allé = I went (one male)

elle est allée = she went

nous sommes allées = we went (two or more females)

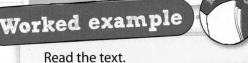

Worked example

READING   target **B**

Read the text.

L'année dernière, en hiver, j'ai fait un stage de ski à l'UCPA avec mon meilleur copain Brice. L'UCPA est une société qui organise des vacances sportives.

Nous avons choisi un stage de ski à La Plagne dans les Alpes. C'était un stage pour les ados de 13 à 17 ans. L'hébergement était dans un chalet énorme. Nous avons partagé notre chambre avec deux autres garçons qui faisaient le même stage.

La nourriture était suffisante mais nous sommes souvent sortis le soir pour aller à la pizzeria parce qu'on avait une faim de loup après la journée sur les pistes.

Answer the question **in English**.

When exactly was the holiday? last winter

Reading carefully

- First read the text through QUICKLY to get an idea of what it's about.
- READ the text again and make sure you understand the tenses, etc.
- Read the QUESTIONS carefully – they should give you clues about the text. Then be precise in how you answer them.

Read the question **carefully** – here you are asked when **exactly** Baptiste went on holiday – you will need to write 'last' + 'winter' to score.

Now try this

READING   target **B**

Read the text again and complete the activity.

(a) Who did Baptiste go on holiday with?

(b) Who was the holiday aimed at?

(c) Give **two** details about the accommodation.

(d) Why did they often go out to eat?

Be **precise** in your answer here – what sort of friend is Brice exactly?

Give **two details** for **two marks**.

Countries

If you are talking about the nationality of someone female, you need to make adjectives agree.

Les pays

	Country	Nationality (adj)
	l'Allemagne (f)	allemand(e)
	l'Angleterre (f)	anglais(e)
	la Belgique	belge
	l'Écosse (f)	écossais(e)
	l'Espagne (f)	espagnol(e)
	les États-Unis (mpl)	américain(e)
	la France	français(e)
	la Grande-Bretagne	britannique
	l'Irlande (f)	irlandais(e)
	le Maroc	marocain(e)
	le pays de Galles	gallois(e)
	la Pologne	polonais(e)
	la Suisse	suisse

'in' + country

To say 'in' with names of countries, use:

masc	fem	plural
au	en	aux

J'habite en Angleterre.
I live in England.

J'ai passé les vacances au pays de Galles.
I spent the holiday in Wales.

Je voudrais étudier aux États-Unis.
I would like to study in the United States.

Most countries are **feminine**.

Write about where you live.

Je suis écossaise. J'habite à Grantham en Angleterre depuis cinq ans mais je suis née à Édimbourg, en Écosse.

AIMING HIGHER Je préfère habiter en Angleterre plutôt qu'en Écosse parce que j'aime l'ambiance ici. L'endroit où j'habite est animé et près de commerces, mais mes amis qui habitent encore en Écosse me manquent beaucoup. Alors cette année, je vais leur rendre visite et ça va être chouette, j'en suis sûr.

This student has included the correct **agreements** on écossaise (Scottish) and **née** (born), as she is a girl.

This student has raised his level by **comparing** the two countries, by using words such as **où** (the place where I live) and looking ahead with the **near future** je vais leur rendre visite (I am going to visit them).

Developing your answer

Always look for opportunities to add more information to your written work. You could:

* say how long you have lived somewhere
* say where you were born (Je suis né(e) à / en …)
* give your opinion.

Write a paragraph of about 100 words, answering these questions:
* Tu es de quelle nationalité?
* Où es-tu né(e)?
* Où habites-tu maintenant? Tu trouves l'endroit comment?
* Où voudrais-tu habiter à l'âge de 21 ans? Pourquoi?

Check your written work for:
* correct endings on adjectives and past participles
* accents on words which need them.

My house

Home, sweet home! You will have met this topic at Key Stage 3 – revise it carefully!

Ma maison

J'habite ...	I live (in) ...
une maison individuelle	a detached house
une maison jumelée	a semi-detached house
une HLM	a council flat / house
un immeuble	a block of flats
au rez-de-chaussée	on the ground floor
au premier étage	on the first floor
au sous-sol	in the basement
Il y a (sept) pièces.	There are (seven) rooms.
cave (f)	cellar
chambre (f)	bedroom
cuisine (f)	kitchen
jardin (m)	garden
meubles (mpl)	furniture
salle à manger (f)	dining room
salle de bains (f)	bathroom
salon (m)	living room

Some useful adjectives:
confortable	comfortable	joli(e)	pretty
pratique	practical		
démodé(e)	old-fashioned		

Adjectives

Grammar page 87

Remember, adjectives agree with the person or thing they describe.

Most adjectives come AFTER the noun:

un appartement moderne
a modern flat

However, a number of common adjectives, like grand and petit, come IN FRONT OF the noun:

un grand immeuble
a big block of flats

 Worked example   READING   target C-D

Read Lafti's text.

Lafti: Notre maison est petite. C'est une HLM. Nous y habitons depuis trois ans. Je l'aime bien! Nous avons une jolie cuisine mais nous n'avons pas de jardin.

Hugo: Nous habitons un grand immeuble en banlieue. Notre appartement est au septième étage donc on a besoin d'un ascenseur. Il y a trois chambres mais il n'y a pas de salle à manger.

Note ...

(a) the type of house / flat that Lafti lives in council house

(b) the room / facility she doesn't have a garden

EXAM ALERT!

In this type of question, you need to note details rather than select from answer options. Make sure you read the question carefully to see what information is being asked for.

 If you write lots of extra information, you may be penalised.

Students have struggled with exam questions similar to this - **be prepared!**

 Now try this   READING   target C-D

Read the other text and complete the activity for Hugo.

	Type of house / flat	Doesn't have
Hugo:		

Signs around town

Look carefully at the vocabulary on this page, as signs around town may crop up in reading questions.

Les panneaux

défense de ...	... is forbidden
interdit de ...	... is forbidden
il est recommandé de ...	... is recommended

sortie de secours
emergency exit

bienvenue
welcome

désolé – fermé
sorry – closed

entrée
entrance

distributeur de billets
cash dispenser

ouvert
open

fermé
closed

visite guidée
guided tour

zone piétonne
pedestrian zone

Days of the week

Days in French don't have a capital letter.

lundi	jeudi
mardi	vendredi
mercredi	samedi
	dimanche

tous les samedis	every Saturday
le samedi	on Saturday(s)
sauf le lundi	except Monday
de mardi à vendredi	from Tuesday to Friday
les jours fériés	public holidays

Worked example

Read these signs.

A Bibliothèque municipale ouverte: 9h – 18h

B Défense de fumer dans la zone piétonne

C Coiffeur Martin
Ouvert tous les jours sauf le dimanche

D Concert au Palais
Il est recommandé d'acheter les billets à l'avance.

E Boulangerie italienne
Fermé pour les vacances d'hiver

Choose the correct answer.

What can't you do in the pedestrian zone?

You can't **smoke** / **go on Sundays** / **throw things** in the pedestrian area.

- You need to locate the correct **sign** and then the correct **message** contained in that sign. The question mentions 'pedestrian zone' so it is easy to spot that the sign you need is B, as it has the cognate **la zone piétonne**.

- You now need to work out **fumer**. If you don't know it, look at the answer options and rule out any you know are definitely wrong. This will help you choose correctly.

Now try this

Read the signs again and choose the correct answers.

(a) The **bakery** / **library** / **concert hall** is closed for the holidays.

(b) You should buy concert tickets **in advance** / **online** / **from the ticket office**.

(c) You can't get your hair cut on **Friday** / **Monday** / **Sunday**.

Opinions of where you live

Using modifiers and adjectives in your speaking and writing will help improve your answers.

Des opinions d'où tu habites

J'aime vivre ici. I like living here.

Il y a beaucoup de choses à faire.
There are a lot of things to do.

On peut faire des achats.
You can go shopping.

C'est pittoresque.
It's picturesque.

C'est une grande ville bruyante.
It is a large noisy town.

Autrefois, on pouvait aller à
la piscine.
You used to be able to go to
the swimming pool.

Aujourd'hui, il n'y a rien à faire.
Today there is nothing to do.

C'est un endroit tranquille et ennuyeux.
It is a quiet and boring area.

Il y a trop de circulation.
There is too much traffic.

Modifiers

assez	quite
beaucoup	much
trop	too (much)
encore	more
un peu	a bit
très	very
plus	more
moins	less
plutôt	rather
vraiment	really

Le centre-ville est **trop** bruyant.
The town centre is too noisy.

Ma ville est
très polluée.
My town is
very polluted.

Worked example

Write about the advantages and disadvantages of where you live.

> J'aime habiter ici parce que c'est pittoresque. Il n'y a pas beaucoup de circulation et il y a beaucoup de choses à faire. En plus, tous mes amis habitent ici.

Avoid overusing the structures **il y a** (there is / are) and **et** (and) to join sentences. This extract uses the **3rd person plural** (mes amis habitent) which helps to raise the level.

AIMING HIGHER

> De nos jours, les avantages de ma ville, c'est qu'on peut faire beaucoup de sports, aller au cinéma et fréquenter des sites touristiques. Mais l'inconvénient, c'est que tout ça coûte cher. Dans ma ville idéale, toutes les distractions seraient gratuites pour les ados et on pourrait aller au centre de sport sans payer.

This answer uses a **variety** of structures and vocabulary, and includes two **conditional** phrases at the end: **seraient gratuites** (would be free) and **on pourrait** (you could) – which raises the level further.

Now try this

Write about the advantages and disadvantages of where you live.

Try to take into account the advice above.

News headlines

Look at the news headlines on a French internet site. You may be surprised at what you CAN understand!

Les gros titres

gaz d'échappement (m)	exhaust fumes
guerre (f)	war
incendie (m) / feu (m)	fire
inondation (f)	flood
marée (f)	tide
mer (f)	sea
paix (f)	peace
paysage (m)	countryside
terre (f)	earth
tremblement de terre (m)	earthquake
vague (f)	wave
détruit(e)	destroyed
entouré(e)	surrounded
inondé(e)	flooded
surpeuplé(e)	overpopulated
tuer	to kill

Prepositions

par	by
avec	with
pour	for
au milieu de	in the middle of
sans	without
jusqu'à	until
parmi	amongst
en dehors de	outside

par un incendie
by a fire

au milieu de la mer
in the middle of the sea

Worked example

  READING / target A-A*

Read the news reports.

> **D**es centaines d'hectares du paysage espagnol ont été détruits par un incendie. La cause n'est pas connue.

> En Syrie il y a un risque de guerre civile après les attaques des derniers jours. Tout espoir de paix est fini pour le moment.

> **S**uite à une marée haute, la petite ville de St Jean de Pierre a été inondée par la mer. Plusieurs habitants on dû quitter leur maison et l'inondation a fait des dégâts sérieux.

Read this sentence and write **T** (true), **F** (false) or **?** (not in the text).

Hundreds of hectares of Spanish countryside are at risk of being destroyed. ☐F☐

Working out words

Use these STRATEGIES to work out unknown words:

- Use OTHER FRENCH WORDS: connu(e) is difficult, but you know that connaître means 'to know'. This helps you to work out that connu means 'known'.
- Look for COGNATES (words like English words): un risque is 'a risk'.
- Use the QUESTION and the CONTEXT: the question on the text about Syria mentions 'peace' – that gives you a context to identify the French for 'peace' and work out the answer.

Now try this

  READING / target A-A*

Read the news reports again. For each sentence below, write **T** (true), **F** (false) or **?** (not in the text).

(a) The cause of the fire was known. ☐

(b) There is hope for peace in Syria. ☐

(c) St Jean de Pierre is often flooded at high tide. ☐

(d) No real damage was done by the flood. ☐

School subjects

You may need to be able to talk about school subjects, give your opinions and justify them.

Les matières

J'apprends / J'étudie ...   I learn / I study ...
J'aime / Je préfère ...   I like / I prefer ...
Je n'aime pas ...   I don't like ...

 l'allemand (m)

 l'anglais (m)

 le dessin

 l'espagnol (m)

 le français

 la biologie

 la chimie

 la physique

 les mathématiques / maths (fpl)

 l'informatique (f)

 la géographie

 l'histoire (f)

 l'instruction religieuse (f)

 l'EPS / éducation physique (f)

Negative sentences

After the negative ne ... pas, use de before the noun.

Je ne fais pas de sport.
I don't do sport.
Je n'ai pas de cours le mercredi.
I don't have lessons on Wednesdays.

depuis + present tense

depuis + present tense = how long you have been doing something
J'apprends le français depuis quatre ans.
I have been learning French for four years.

EPS – 'e' is pronounced 'uh': 'uh pay ess'.
EMT – 'uh em tay'. (EMT / éducation manuelle et technique (f) = DT in English)
Subject names are often abbreviated: info, bio, géo.

Worked example SPEAKING

Tu aimes quelles matières?

J'apprends l'espagnol depuis deux ans, mais je n'aime pas cette langue parce que c'est trop compliqué et je n'aime pas le prof.

AIMING HIGHER
Personnellement, je n'aime pas trop le dessin parce que je ne m'y intéresse pas, ce n'est pas mon truc. En revanche, j'adore le sport. C'est rigolo et d'habitude, on en fait deux heures par semaine. Mon sport préféré, c'est le basket et ce qu'il y a de mieux, c'est qu'on peut y jouer dans une équipe, même si on n'est pas très doué. Quand j'irai au lycée, je vais continuer le basket mais j'espère aussi faire de l'escalade.

Say **how long** you have been doing a subject, using **depuis**, and then go on to give your **opinion** plus **reasons** for your opinion.

This student expresses a **range of ideas** and **points of view**. As well as using more than one tense, he includes a variety of **interesting** vocabulary and structures, including the adverbs **personnellement**, **d'habitude** and **trop**, and the phrases **en revanche** (on the other hand), **ce n'est pas mon truc** (it's not my thing) and **ce qu'il y a de mieux, c'est ...** (the best thing is ...).

Now try this SPEAKING

Answer these questions. Say two sentences about each.
- Quelle est ta matière préférée? Pourquoi?
- Est-ce qu'il y a une matière que tu n'aimes pas?

Opinions of school

In listening and reading tasks you will often have to understand opinions, not just key words.

Des opinions de l'école

devoirs (mpl)	homework
directeur (m) / directrice (f)	head teacher
élève (m/f)	pupil
études (fpl)	studies
étudiant(e) (m/f)	student
examen (m)	exam
instruction civique (f)	PSHCE
langues étrangères / vivantes (fpl)	foreign / modern languages
note (f)	mark
professeur (m)	teacher
sport (m)	sport
bien / mal équipé(e)	well / badly equipped
difficile	difficult
doué(e)	gifted
facile	easy
travailleur / travailleuse	hard-working
échouer	to fail
redoubler	to resit a year
Je suis fort(e) en maths.	I am strong in maths.
Il est faible en dessin.	He is weak in art.

'first', 'second', 'third'

premier is the only ordinal number to change in the feminine form:

	masculine	feminine
1st	premier	première
2nd	deuxième	deuxième
3rd	troisième	troisième

le premier cours   the first lesson

la première leçon   the first lesson

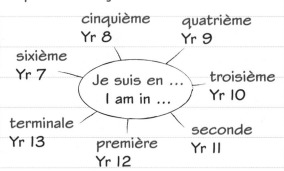

- sixième — Yr 7
- cinquième — Yr 8
- quatrième — Yr 9
- troisième — Yr 10
- seconde — Yr 11
- première — Yr 12
- terminale — Yr 13

Je suis en ... / I am in ...

Worked example

LISTENING 36   target B-C

Who says what about school?

Write **A** (for Amélie), **D** (for Damien) or **N** (for Nicolas).

(a) Who says their school is well equipped? ☐ A

(b) Who does not want to resit the year? ☐

(c) Who usually has good marks? ☐

(d) Who complains about too much homework? ☐

(e) Who would like to work abroad? ☐

– On fait un sondage. D'abord, Amélie. Que penses-tu de ton collège?

– J'ai de la chance car mon collège est très bien équipé. Mais le travail est dur et les profs nous donnent trop de devoirs. La matière que je préfère, c'est l'instruction civique car on discute de choses intéressantes!

- You need to listen carefully from the **very beginning** – if you miss the speaker's name, it will be tricky.
- It is not enough to just identify a **key word**, as you also need to identify the **opinion** that goes with it. For example, for question d, two speakers mention **les devoirs** (homework) but you are only interested in the person who says they have **too much**.

Now try this

LISTENING 37   target B-C

Listen to the whole recording and complete the activity.

School routine

You may want to write about school routine in your writing assessment. Make sure your verbs are correct.

La routine au collège

car de ramassage (m)	school bus
cour (f)	playground
cours (m) / leçon (f)	lesson
grandes vacances (fpl)	summer holidays
heure du déjeuner (f)	lunch break
pause (f)	break
récréation / récré (f)	break
rentrée (f)	start of the new school year
retenue (f)	detention
trimestre (m)	term
commencer	to begin
comprendre	to understand
durer	to last
faire des progrès	to make progress
finir	to finish
le matin	in the morning
l'après-midi	in the afternoon
pas d'école	no school

Third person plural

The 3rd person singular (he / she) and plural (they) of most verbs sound the same but you have to SPELL them correctly.

singular (he)	plural (they)
il commence	ils commencent
il rentre	ils rentrent

Irregular 3rd person plural forms:

aller	to go	ils vont	they go
avoir	to have	ils ont	they have
être	to be	ils sont	they are
faire	to do	ils font	they do

Les cours finissent à quatre heures.
Lessons finish at four o'clock.

Worked example

Describe your typical school day.

Le matin, les cours commencent à huit heures et finissent à midi vingt. Un cours dure une heure. Nous avons une heure quarante pour le déjeuner et puis les cours recommencent à deux heures.

AIMING HIGHER

Le mardi, les cours ne commencent qu'à dix heures. Les élèves comme moi, qui prennent un car de ramassage, arrivent au collège à huit heures. Pendant la récré, on va normalement dans la cour pour bavarder, mais hier, je suis allée à la bibliothèque parce qu'il me fallait finir mes devoirs de dessin. Je déteste le dessin parce que je trouve les devoirs très difficiles et ennuyeux.

This is adequate, but is all in **one tense**. To get a higher grade you need to use a **past** or **future** tense as well as the **present**, and include an **opinion**.

- This uses an **interesting structure** to begin with: **les cours ne commencent qu'à** (lessons don't begin until) which makes a good start. It also includes the **perfect tense** by describing a specific event from yesterday.

- The expression **il me fallait** + infinitive (I had to) is the sort of structure that will help you aim for a top grade.

Now try this

Write a paragraph of about 100 words about your school routine.

- When do lessons start and finish?
- What do you do at break and lunchtime?

Articles 2

It is crucial that you can use du, de la, de l' or des to say 'some', and au, à la, à l' or aux to say 'to the'.

How to say 'some'

masculine	feminine	beginning with vowel or silent h	plural
du	de la	de l'	des

le lait   the milk ➡ du lait   some milk

la confiture   jam   ➡ de la confiture   some jam

l'essence   petrol   ➡ de l'essence   some petrol

les animaux   animals ➡ des animaux   some animals

But after the negative you only use de / d':

Je n'ai pas de pain.   I haven't any bread.

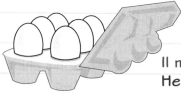

Il n'a pas d'œufs.
He hasn't any eggs.

- We don't always need to use 'some' in English. Sometimes we miss it out altogether, but you HAVE to use it in French:

  Veux-tu du lait ou du café?
  Do you want milk or coffee?

- And in English, when we ask a question we use 'any':

  Avez-vous des boissons?
  Have you got any drinks?

  Avez-vous du pain?
  Have you got any bread?

How to say 'to the'

masculine	feminine	beginning with vowel or silent h	plural
au	à la	à l'	aux

au bureau   to the office

à la mairie   to the town hall

à l'école   to (the) school

aux toilettes   to the toilets

On va au collège.

Now try this

1 How would you tell someone how to go to these places using **aller**? For example, **Allez au carrefour**.

(a) [..........................] parking (m)

(b) [..........................] toilettes (pl)

(c) [..........................] gare (f)

(d) [..........................] arrêt de bus (m)

(e) [..........................] feux (pl)

(f) [..........................] supermarché (m)

(g) [..........................] château (m)

(h) [..........................] tour Eiffel (f)

2 Translate these phrases into French.

(a) I want some bread.

(b) Have you got any milk?

(c) He hasn't got any petrol.

(d) I'm going to school.

(e) Are you going to the town hall?

(f) He's going to the toilets.

You have all the vocabulary you need on the page!

Adjectives

When using adjectives, you have to think about AGREEMENT and POSITION.

Regular adjectives

- Adjectives must agree with the noun they are describing. Regular adjectives add -e for feminine, -s for masculine plural and -es for feminine plural.

singular		plural	
masc	fem	masc	fem
grand	grande	grands	grandes
petit	petite	petits	petites

- Some adjectives already end in -e so don't add another:

masc	fem	masc plural	fem plural
timide	timide	timides	timides

- And some are a little less regular:

masc	fem	masc plural	fem plural	
long	longue	longs	longues	long
blanc	blanche	blancs	blanches	white
sec	sèche	secs	sèches	dry

A very few adjectives don't change at all e.g:

marron   chestnut
orange   orange

Irregular adjectives

- Adjectives which end in -x, change their ending to -se in the feminine:

singular		plural	
masc	fem	masc	fem
sérieux	sérieuse	sérieux	sérieuses

Other adjectives like sérieux:
dangereux   dangerous
merveilleux   marvellous
heureux   fortunate

- Adjectives which end in -f change to -ve in the feminine:

singular		plural	
masc	fem	masc	fem
actif	active	actifs	actives

Other adjectives like actif:
sportif   sporty   positif   positive

- Adjectives which end in -er change to -ère in the feminine:

premier ➡ première   first
dernier ➡ dernière   last

- Adjectives which end in -on, -en or -il double the consonant before adding -e: in the feminine:

mignon   ➡   mignonne   nice
gentil   ➡   gentille   kind

Postition of adjectives

Most adjectives come AFTER the noun:

les yeux bleus   les cheveux longs

There are a few common adjectives which come IN FRONT OF the noun:

grand(e)	big	vieux / vieille	old
petit(e)	small	nouveau / nouvelle	new
joli(e)	pretty	meilleur(e)	best

mon meilleur ami
my best friend

ma meilleure amie
my best friend

Now try this

Translate these phrases into French.

1 a little black dog
2 last week
3 My little brother is very active.

4 My best friend (f) is small and shy.
5 Her brother is tall, sporty but a bit serious.

-IR and -RE verbs

There are two groups of -ir verbs: those which take -ss in the plural forms and those which don't.

-ir verbs which take -ss

FINIR   TO FINISH

je	finis	nous finissons
tu	finis	vous finissez
il / elle / on finit		ils / elles finissent

Verbs like finir:

choisir   to choose

By now you will have noticed that the je, tu and il / elle forms of most verbs sound the same BUT they are not all spelled the same, so be careful when you are writing!

-ir verbs which don't take -ss

PARTIR   TO LEAVE

je pars	nous partons
tu pars	vous partez
il / elle / on part	ils / elles partent

Verbs like partir:

dormir   to sleep (je dors)

sortir   to go out (je sors)

-ir verbs are sometimes referred to as -s -s -t verbs. Can you think of a reason why?

-re verbs

RÉPONDRE   TO REPLY

je réponds	nous répondons
tu réponds	vous répondez
il / elle / on répond	ils / elles répondent

Verbs like répondre:

attendre	to wait
vendre	to sell
entendre	to hear
perdre	to lose
descendre	to go down

Irregular -re verbs

DIRE   TO SAY

je dis	nous disons
tu dis	vous dites
il / elle / on dit	ils / elles disent

Verbs like dire:

lire   to read BUT nous lisons, vous lisez

écrire to write BUT écrivons, écrivez, écrivent

boire to drink BUT buvons, buvez, boivent

prendre (to take), comprendre (to understand) and apprendre (to learn) are regular except for the nous, vous and ils/elles forms:

je prends	nous prenons
tu prends	vous prenez
il / elle / on prend	ils / elles prennent

Now try this

Complete these sentences with the correct part of the verb in brackets.

1 Le matin je (sortir) à sept heures et demie.
2 Le mardi les cours (finir) à cinq heures.
3 Mon copain et moi ne (boire) pas de coca.
4 Le train (partir) à 8h20.
5 Nous (apprendre) l'espagnol.
6 Pendant les vacances, nous (dormir) sous la tente.
7 Mes copains (choisir) des frites.

Je dors sous
la tente.

avoir and être

TO HAVE (avoir) and TO BE (être) are two of the most common verbs used in French. They are both IRREGULAR, so you need to learn their different parts really carefully.

avoir

j'ai	I have
tu as	you have (informal)
il a	he has
nous avons	we have
vous avez	you have (formal)
ils ont	they have

When to use avoir

In French you use avoir to describe your age, or to say that you HAVE hunger or fear or cold.

J'ai seize ans.	I am 16 years old.
J'ai faim.	I am hungry.
Il a peur des fantômes.	He is afraid of ghosts.
J'ai froid.	I am cold.

être

Je suis	I am
tu es	you are (informal)
il est	he is
nous sommes	we are
vous êtes	you are (formal)
ils sont	they are

The most common mistake with être is to add it when you are using other verbs. Don't just replace 'am' with suis.

je parle	I am talking
nous allons	we are going

Useful phrases with avoir and être

J'ai trois frères.	I have three brothers.
Vous avez tort.	You're wrong.
J'ai mal à la tête.	I have a headache.
J'ai besoin d'un stylo.	I need a pen.
Je suis anglais(e).	I am English.
La table est marron.	The table is brown.
Nous sommes frères.	We are brothers.
Ils sont étudiants.	They are students.

Auxiliary verbs

Avoir and être are both used as AUXILIARY VERBS. This means they are used to make other TENSES. You can use the present tense of avoir and être to make the perfect tense. Don't forget to make agreements with être.

J'ai mangé.	I have eaten.
Nous avons payé.	We have paid.
Je suis allé(e).	I have gone (or I went).
Il est parti.	He has left.

Now try this

1 Complete this passage. All the missing words are parts of the verb avoir.

Nous .... un petit chaton. Il est tout noir mais il .... les yeux verts. Il .... toujours faim. Il .... beaucoup de jouets mais j'.......... une balle de ping pong qu'il adore et mon petit frère .... un petit oiseau en fourrure qu'il dechire. .... -tu un animal?

2 Complete this passage. All the missing words are parts of the verb être.

Je .... britannique. Je .... né en Angleterre. Mes parents .... italiens. Ils .... nés en Italie mais ils habitent ici depuis vingt ans. Mon frère .... sportif. Il .... champion régional de judo. Ma sœur .... paresseuse. En revanche je .... charmant!

You can replace mes parents with ils and the sentence still makes sense. So the right part of the verb here is mes parents sont.

The perfect tense 2

Most verbs form the perfect tense with avoir BUT some verbs use être instead. They are mostly verbs to do with movement.

Verbs which take être

The following 14 verbs take être + the past participle in the perfect tense:

aller / venir	to go / to come
arriver / partir	to arrive / to depart
entrer / sortir	to enter / to leave
monter / descendre	to go up / to go down
rester / tomber	to stay / to fall
naître / mourir	to be born / to die
rentrer / revenir	to return

ALL reflexive verbs also take être.

MRS VAN DER TRAMP spells out the first letters of the 14 verbs listed above and may be useful in helping you to remember them!

Formation

ÊTRE:	+	PAST PARTICIPLES:
je suis		allé / venu
tu es		arrivé / parti
il / elle / on est		entré / sorti
nous sommes		monté / descendu
vous êtes		né / mort
ils / elles sont		rentré / revenu

Note how the past participle changes according to who is doing the action:

Je suis allé(e).	I went.
Elle est arrivée.	She arrived.
Nous sommes monté(e)s.	We climbed.
Ils sont partis.	They left.

Agreement of the past participle

With verbs which take être, the past participle agrees with the subject of the verb (a bit like adjectives):

Je suis allé(e)
Tu es allé(e)
Il est allé
Elle est allée
Nous sommes allé(e)s
Vous êtes allé(e)(s)
Ils sont allés
Elles sont allées

Aiming higher

- You should be able to use the perfect tense if you are aiming at a higher grade.
- Remember, you use the perfect tense when you are talking about ONE SPECIFIC time in the past, so you are likely to start the sentence with a time expression referring to the past.

For example:

Samedi dernier ...	Last Saturday ...
Hier ...	Yesterday ...
Hier soir ...	Last night ...
Il y a deux jours ...	Two days ago ...
Pendant les vacances ...	During the holidays ...

Now try this

Put the infinitives in brackets into the perfect tense to complete the sentences.

1 Samedi dernier je (se lever) de bonne heure.
2 Le matin je (aller) jouer au football.
3 Je (sortir) à dix heures.
4 L'autre équipe (ne pas venir).
5 Nous y (rester) une heure, puis nous (rentrer).
6 Je (arriver) à la maison juste avant midi.

Je suis allé(e) au match.

The imperfect tense

The imperfect is another verb tense you use to talk about the past.

Forming the imperfect

First, take the nous form of the present tense and remove the -ons ending:

nous habit~~ons~~

Then add the following imperfect endings:

je -ais	nous -ions
tu -ais	vous -iez
il / elle / on -ait	ils / elles -aient

HABITER TO LIVE

j'habitais	nous habitions
tu habitais	vous habitiez
il / elle / on habitait	ils / elles habitaient

Good news: all verbs except **être** are regular in the imperfect tense.

Using the imperfect

You use the imperfect tense to describe:

1 What WAS HAPPENING:
  Il pleuvait.   It was raining.

2 What USED TO happen:
  Quand j'étais jeune, je jouais au foot.
  When I was young, I used to play football.

3 What was ONGOING when something else happened:
  Je regardais la télévision, lorsque quelqu'un a sonné.   I was watching TV when someone rang.

The key words to look out for are: 'was / were ...ing' and 'used to ...'.

Some common verbs

These are a few common verbs you should be able to use in the imperfect.

Present	Imperfect	English
voul/ons	je voul+ais	I wanted
av/ons	j'av+ais	I had
all/ons	j'all+ais	I was going
buv/ons	je buv+ais	I was drinking
mange/ons	je mange+ais	I was eating
achet/ons	j'achet+ais	I was buying
finiss/ons	je finiss+ais	I was finishing
dorm/ons	je dorm+ais	I was sleeping

être in the imperfect

The only IRREGULAR verb in the imperfect tense is être. The stem is ét- and you add the normal imperfect endings to this stem:

j'étais	I was
tu étais	you were
il / elle / on était	he / she / one was
nous étions	we were
vous étiez	you were
ils / elles étaient	they were

Now try this

Complete the text with the imperfect tense of the verbs in the box, then translate it into English.

Why is it written in the imperfect tense?

Quand j'.................................. jeune j'.................................. à la campagne. Nous .... un grand jardin où je .... au foot avec mes frères. Le samedi on .... au marché en ville. Il y .... beaucoup de vendeurs de fruits et légumes et un kiosque à journaux où j'.................................. des bonbons. Nous ……..… des merguez (des saucisses épicées) et nous .... du coca. On .... en bus avec tous nos voisins et nos achats!

avoir   être   habiter   jouer   aller   acheter   manger   boire   rentrer

The future tense

To aim for a high grade you need to use the future tense as well as the present and past!

Near future tense

When you are talking about what you are GOING to do, use the verb to go (aller) + an infinitive, just as in English:

Je vais aller ...   I am going to go ...

Ils vont jouer au tennis.
They are going to play tennis.

Mon copain va rentrer à 21h00.
My friend is going to go home at 9 o'clock.

On va se retrouver en ville.
We are going to meet in town.

Remember all the parts of aller (to go):

je vais	nous allons	
tu vas	vous allez	+ infinitive
il / elle / on va	ils / elles vont	

Remember, the INFINITIVE is the part of the verb you will find in the dictionary – usually ending in -er, -ir or -re.
For example:
-er: jouer / manger
-ir: finir / choisir / sortir
-re: lire / dire

Future tense

If you are aiming for a top grade, you will need to be able to understand and use the 'proper' future. It is used to say what you WILL do.

The future is made from the INFINITIVE + FUTURE TENSE ENDINGS:

-er verbs	manger	➡ je mangerai	I will eat
-ir verbs	finir	➡ je finirai	I will finish
-re verbs	répondre	➡ je répondrai	I will reply

The future ENDINGS are the same as the present tense of avoir except for the nous and vous forms:

je mangerai	nous mangerons
tu mangeras	vous mangerez
il / elle / on mangera	ils / elles mangeront

Which future to use?

NEAR FUTURE (futur proche):
I AM GOING TO PLAY football tonight.
This is a simple fact.

PROPER FUTURE (futur):
I WILL PLAY football tonight.

You might be:
• expressing an intention.
• responding to a suggestion that you might not do something.

Je jouerai au babyfoot au café.

Irregular verbs

BE CAREFUL! There are a few common verbs which don't use the infinitive, but have an irregular stem. The good news is the endings are always the same.

aller	irai	I will go
avoir	aurai	I will have
être	serai	I will be
faire	ferai	I will do
pouvoir	pourrai	I will be able to
venir	viendrai	I will come
voir	verrai	I will see
vouloir	voudrai	I will want

Now try this

Put all the infinitives in brackets into the future tense to complete the text.

L'année prochaine nous (aller) en France. Nous (prendre) l'Eurostar. On (partir) de Londres et on (arriver) à Paris. Puis on (changer) de train et on (continuer) vers le sud. Nous (faire) du camping. Mes parents (dormir) dans une caravane mais je (dormir) sous une tente. Pendant la journée nous (aller) sur la plage et (jouer) au basket et au tennis. Le soir on (manger) au resto. On (se faire) des amis.

The conditional

You should know a few verbs in the conditional and be able to use them in your writing and speaking in order to aim for a higher mark.

The conditional

The conditional is used to say what you WOULD do:

je voudrais – I would like
je jouerais – I would play

It is also used for making suggestions:

on pourrait ... – we could ...

The conditional is formed in a similar way to the future. It uses the same stem (usually the infinitive) but then adds the same endings as the imperfect tense:

manger ➡ je mangerais I would eat
finir   ➡ je finirais   I would finish
vendre ➡ je vendrais   I would sell

You may meet the conditional after si (if):

Si + imperfect tense + conditional

Si tu mangeais correctement, tu n'aurais plus faim.

If you ate properly you wouldn't be hungry.

Irregular conditionals

Irregular conditionals use the same stems as the the irregular future:

Infinitive	Conditional	English
aller	j'irais	I would go
avoir	j'aurais	I would have
être	je serais	I would be
faire	je ferais	I would do
pouvoir	je pourrais	I would be able to
venir	je viendrais	I would come
voir	je verrais	I would see
vouloir	je voudrais	I would like

The endings are always the same:

je mangerais   nous mangerions
tu mangerais   vous mangeriez
il / elle mangerait   ils / elles mangeraient

Je voudrais aller au concert ce soir.
I'd like to go to the concert this evening.

On pourrait faire du bowling?
We could go bowling?

Now try this

Put the infinitives in the following sentences in the conditional.

1 Je (vouloir) aller en Italie.
2 Si j'avais assez d'argent, j'(aller) en Inde.
3 Nous (pouvoir) faire un long voyage.
4 Tu (aimer) voir ce film?
5 Je (préférer) manger au restaurant.
6 Si j'avais faim, je (manger) une pizza.
7 Il (vouloir) aller en ville samedi.
8 On (pouvoir) aller à la patinoire cet après-midi?
9 Tu (voir) le match si tu restais encore deux jours.
10 Vous (vouloir) quelque chose à boire?

The pluperfect tense

The pluperfect is another past tense. You don't have to USE it at GCSE but you should be able to RECOGNISE it. It is used to say what you HAD done.

The pluperfect tense

You use the pluperfect to talk about an event that took place one step further back than another past event.

Whereas the perfect tense means 'I did something' or 'I have done something', the pluperfect is used to say what you HAD done.

We HAD finished dinner (pluperfect) when she knocked on the door. (perfect)

J'avais déjà mangé quand je suis allé au cinéma.
I had already eaten when I went to the cinema.

How does it work?

The pluperfect is formed like the perfect tense with the auxiliary (avoir or être) + the past participle.

The difference is that it uses the IMPERFECT of the auxiliary:

J'avais déjà mangé.   I had already eaten.

J'étais allé(e) en ville. I had gone into town.

The verbs which take être are the same ones which take être in the perfect tense (see page 102). Remember MRS VAN DER TRAMP.

Also remember that the past participle of être verbs must agree with the subject.

Mes parents étaient partis en vacances et j'étais seul à la maison.

My parents had gone on holiday and I was alone in the house.

The pluperfect with avoir

Here is an avoir verb in the pluperfect:

j'avais mangé	I had eaten
tu avais mangé	you had eaten
il / elle / on avait mangé	he / she / one had eaten
nous avions mangé	we had eaten
vous aviez mangé	you had eaten
ils / elles avaient mangé	they had eaten

The pluperfect with être

Here is an être verb in the pluperfect:

j'étais allé(e)	I had gone
tu étais allé(e)	you had gone
il / on était allé	he / one had gone
elle / on était allé(e)	she / one had gone
nous étions allé(e)s	we had gone
vous étiez allé(e)(s)	you had gone
ils étaient allés	they had gone
elles étaient allées	they had gone

Now try this

Look at the verbs in the highlighted expressions. What tense are they in: pluperfect, imperfect or perfect?

Pendant les vacances de neige, mes parents (1) avaient loué un appartement près des pistes de ski.

(2) J'avais toujours voulu apprendre à faire du ski.

Ma sœur (3) avait déjà fait un stage, mais moi, (4) je n'en avais jamais fait.

(5) J'avais passé des heures devant mon ordinateur pour choisir le meilleur équipement.

(6) J'avais regardé des DVD d'apprentissage de ski. (7) Je savais, en principe, comment descendre des pistes de toutes les couleurs, mais le premier jour (8) je suis sorti et plouf … (9) je suis tombé et (10) je me suis cassé la jambe. (11) Je ne m'attendais pas à passer les vacances à l'hôpital!

Negatives

You need to be able to understand and use negatives to aim for a higher grade in all parts of your exam.

Negative expressions

ne … pas	not
ne … jamais	never
ne … plus	no longer, not any more
ne … rien	nothing, not anything
ne … personne	nobody, not anybody
ne … guère	hardly
ne … aucun(e)	not any
ne … que	only
ne … ni … ni …	neither … nor

Formation

You know that negatives are made by making a ne … pas sandwich around the verb.

The ne is a marker to tell you that a negative is coming …

NE   verb   PAS

Word order

* Personne can also come in front of the verb:

  Personne n'est venu.

  No one came.

* When the verb has two parts, the negative forms the sandwich around the auxiliary:

  Je ne suis jamais allé(e) en France.

  I have never been to France.

* If there is a pronoun before the auxiliary it is included in the sandwich:

  Je n'y suis jamais allé(e).

  I've never been there.

* If there are two verbs, the sandwich goes around the first verb:

  Je ne veux pas y aller.

  I don't want to go there.

  Nous ne pouvons pas télécharger l'appli sans un mot de passe.

  We can't download the app without a password.

* If there is a reflexive pronoun, that is included in the sandwich too:

  Ils ne s'entendent pas bien.

  They don't get on well.

Now try this

1 Match the French negative sentences with the English ones on the right.

   1 Il ne mange pas de viande.
   2 On m'a dit que tu ne fumes plus.
   3 Manon n'a jamais mangé d'escargots.
   4 Nous ne voulons plus rien.
   5 Je n'ai vu personne.
   6 Elle n'a aucun doute.
   7 Il n'a que dix ans.
   8 D'où vient-elle? Elle n'est ni italienne ni espagnole.

   a We don't want anything else.
   b Manon has never eaten snails.
   c I didn't see anyone.
   d He's only ten.
   e She has no doubts.
   f Someone told me you don't smoke any more.
   g Where's she from? She's neither Italian nor Spanish.
   h He doesn't eat meat.

2 Make negative sentences with the expressions provided.

   (a) Tu fais (ne … rien).
   (b) Tu m'as aidé à la maison (ne … jamais).
   (c) Tu fais tes devoirs (ne … plus).
   (d) Tu respectes (ne … personne).
   (e) Tu fais le nécessaire (ne … que).
   (f) Tu peux aller au football ou au restaurant ce soir (ne … ni … ni).

Questions

You won't get very far if you can't ask questions, so make sure you know how to!

Ways of asking questions

You can ask a 'yes' and 'no' question in three ways:

1 Change a statement into a question by raising your voice at the end of the sentence:

Tu vas en ville?

This is the most popular way.

2 Put est-ce que at the start of the sentence ('is it that ...?').

Est-ce que tu vas en ville?

This is probably the easiest way.

3 Swap around the subject and verb.

Vas-tu en ville?

Va-t-il en ville?

This is not used as much as it used to be. You should be able to recognise it but you won't be expected to use it.

Qu'est-ce que tu fais?

Question words

The other way to ask a question is to start with a question word:

Qui?	Who?
Quand?	When?
Où?	Where?
Comment?	How?
Combien de?	How many?
À quelle heure?	At what time?
Pourquoi?	Why?
Que?	What?
Depuis quand?	Since when?

Question words can be followed by est-ce que:

Où est-ce que tu habites?
Where do you live?

Comment est-ce que tu vas au collège?
How do you get to school?

À quelle heure est-ce que tu te lèves?
What time do you get up?

Pourquoi est-ce que tu ne te lèves pas plus tôt?
Why don't you get up earlier?

Depuis quand est-ce que tu habites ici?
How long have you lived here?

Qu'est-ce que tu aimes faire?
What do you like doing?

Now try this

Match up the two parts of each question so that they make sense. Then translate the questions into English.

Où	apprends-tu le français?
Qui	rentrent tes parents?
Comment	voulez-vous faire?
Combien	allez-vous?
À quelle heure	travaille ton père?
Pourquoi	as-tu raté le bus?
Que	d'amis as-tu sur Facebook?
Depuis quand	va à la fête?

Useful little words

Prepositions and conjunctions are very useful little words for making your speaking and writing clear and accurate.

Prepositions

Some prepositions tell you WHERE something is:

à côté de	beside
dans	in
derrière	behind
devant	in front of
dehors	outside
en face de	opposite
entre	between
loin de	far from
près de	near to
partout	everywhere
sous	under
sur	on
vers	towards

Others are just useful little words:

à	at / to
avec	with
chez	at the house of ...
en	in / at
environ	about
jusqu'à	up to / until
sans	without
sauf	except

Note that the de changes to du, de la, de l' or des, depending on the noun that follows.

à côté du cinéma	next to the cinema
en face de la gare	opposite the station
près de l'école	near to the school
près des magasins	near to the shops

Verbs with prepositions

Some common verbs take a preposition before another infinitive:

décider de sortir	to decide to go out
apprendre à conduire	to learn to drive
réussir à faire ...	to succeed in doing ...
oublier de faire ...	to forget to do ...

Saying 'in' or 'to' with places

To say 'in' or 'to' a town or country:

• Use en before the names of feminine countries (most countries are feminine):
  Elle va en France.   She's going to France.

• Use au before masculine countries:
  J'habite au pays de Galles.   I live in Wales.

• Use à before the name of a town:
  J'habite à Paris.   I live in Paris.

Useful conjunctions

Use conjunctions to combine short sentences.

d'abord	at first	aussi	also / as well	puis	then	et	and
au début	at the start	donc	so / then	ensuite	next	mais	but
alors	then	à la fin	at the end	ou	or		

Now try this

Choose a suitable preposition or conjunction from the box to fill each gap.

Je me sentais triste. Mon chat avait disparu! J'avais cherché (1) .... J'avais cherché (2) .... le lit, (3) .... le placard, (4) .... la porte. (5) .... j'ai eu une idée, je suis allé (6) .... et j'ai cherché (7) .... le jardin, mais (8) .... succès. (9) .... je suis rentré (10) .... ma chambre. Je suis allé (11) .... lit. Je l'ai vu! Il était (12) .... les draps.

sous	puis	dans	au	sans	à	partout	à la fin	dehors	dans	sous	dans	derrière

Useful bits and pieces

Numbers

1	un	11	onze	21	vingt-et-un
2	deux	12	douze	22	vingt-deux
3	trois	13	treize	23	vingt-trois
4	quatre	14	quatorze	24	vingt-quatre
5	cinq	15	quinze	25	vingt-cinq
6	six	16	seize	26	vingt-six
7	sept	17	dix-sept	27	vingt-sept
8	huit	18	dix-huit	28	vingt-huit
9	neuf	19	dix-neuf	29	vingt-neuf
10	dix	20	vingt	30	trente

40	quarante	100	cent
50	cinquante	200	deux-cents
60	soixante	1000	mille
70	soixante-dix	2000	deux-mille
80	quatre-vingts		
90	quatre-vingt-dix		

Dates and festivals

Days of the week

lundi mardi mercredi jeudi vendredi samedi dimanche

Months of the year

janvier février mars avril mai juin juillet août septembre octobre novembre décembre

The seasons

le printemps   l'été   l'automne   l'hiver

le premier juin	1st June
le deux avril	2nd April
le trente-et-un mars	31st March
les jours fériés	holidays
Noël	Christmas
le Nouvel An	New Year
la Saint-Sylvestre	New Year's Eve
Pâques	Easter

Intensifiers

très:	very
Il est très grand.	He is very big.
un peu:	a bit
Elle est un peu timide.	She's a bit shy.
trop:	too
Nous sommes trop fatigués.	We are too tired.
assez:	quite
J'ai assez mangé.	I'm full. (I've eaten enough.)
beaucoup	much / many
Merci beaucoup.	Many thanks.

Time

Quelle heure est-il?   What time is it?

Il est huit heures et demie.

Il est neuf heures et quart.

Il est dix heures moins le quart.

Il est midi/minuit.

Quantities

assez de	enough (of)		une boîte de	a box/tin of
beaucoup de	much / many (of)		une bouteille de	a bottle of
plusieurs	several		une cannette	a (drinks) can
un morceau de	a piece of		une douzaine de	a dozen (of)
un paquet de	a packet of		une tranche de	a slice of
un pot de	a jar / tub of		un kilo de	a kilo of
un tiers de	a third of		une livre de	half a kilo of
une moitié de	a half of		un régime de bananes	a bunch of bananas

Vocabulary

These pages cover key French vocabulary that you need to know. This section starts with general terms that are useful in a wide variety of situations and then divides into vocabulary for each of the four main topics covered in this revision guide:

1 General vocabulary   **2** Lifestyle   **3** Leisure
4 Home and environment   **5** Work and education

F Sections to be learnt by **all** candidates   **H** Sections to be learnt by Higher candidates only

Learning vocabulary is essential preparation for your reading and listening exams. Don't try to learn too much at once – concentrate on learning and testing yourself on a page at a time.

1 General vocabulary

Comparative and superlative of adjectives and adverbs

plus	more
moins	less
plus que	more than
moins que	less than
bon	good
meilleur	better
le meilleur	best
mauvais	bad
pire	worse
le pire	worst

Conjunctions and connectives

à cause de	because of
à part	apart from
alors	so, then
aussi	also
car	because
cependant	however
c'est-à-dire	that is (to say)
comme	as
d'un côté / de l'autre côté	on the one hand / on the other hand
donc	so
ensuite	then
et	and
évidemment	of course
mais	but
même si	even if
ou	or
parce que	because
par contre	on the other hand
par exemple	for example
pendant que	while
pourtant	however
puis	then
puisque	since

quand	when
sans doute	without doubt
si	if
y compris	including

Prepositions

à	at, to, in
à côté de	next to
à travers	through
au bord de	on the edge of
au bout de	at the end of
au-dessous de	below
au-dessus de	above
au fond de	at the bottom of
au lieu de	instead of
au milieu de	in the middle of
autour de	around
avec	with
contre	against
dans	in
de	of, from
depuis	since
derrière	behind
devant	in front of
en	in
en dehors de	outside
en face de	opposite
entre	between
jusqu'à	until
malgré	in spite of
parmi	among
pour	for, in order to
près de	near
sans	without
selon	according to
sous	under
sur	on
vers	towards

Negatives

ne... jamais	never
ne... pas	not
ne... personne	no one
ne... plus	no longer
ne... que	only
ne... rien	nothing
ni... ni	neither... nor
pas encore	not yet

Asking questions

combien?	how much / many?
comment?	how?
où?	where?
pourquoi?	why?
quand?	when?
que?	what?
quel / quelle? (m/f)	what, which
qu'est-ce que?	what?
qu'est-ce qui?	who?
qu'est-ce que c'est?	what is it?
qui?	who?
quoi?	what?

Common questions

à quelle heure?	at what time?
ça s'écrit comment?	how do you spell that?
c'est combien?	how much is it?
c'est quelle date?	what date is it?
c'est quel jour?	what day is it?
de quelle couleur?	what colour is it?
d'où?	from where?
où ça?	where is that?
où est ...?	where is ...?
pour combien de temps?	for how long?
que veut dire ...?	what does ... mean?
quelle heure est-il?	what time is it?

Now try this

Practise connectives and prepositions by covering up the English column and then writing down the English translations yourself. Compare your answers with the list above. How many have you got right?

❶ General vocabulary

Greetings and exclamations

à bientôt	see you soon
à demain	see you tomorrow
à tout à l'heure	see you later
allô	hello
amitiés	regards
au revoir	goodbye
au secours	help
bien sûr	of course
bienvenue	welcome
bonjour	hello / good morning
bon anniversaire	happy birthday
bon appétit	enjoy your meal
bon voyage	have a good trip
bonne année	happy new year
bonne chance	good luck
bonne idée	good idea
bonne nuit	goodnight
bonnes vacances	have a good holiday
bonsoir	good evening
ça va?	how are you?
d'accord	agreed / OK
de rien	don't mention it
désolé(e)	sorry
excusez-moi	excuse me
félicitations	congratulations
joyeux Noël	happy Christmas
meilleurs vœux	best wishes
quel dommage	what a pity
salut	hi
santé	cheers
s'il te / vous plaît	please

Opinions

à mon avis	in my opinion
absolument	absolutely
affreux/euse	awful
agréable	pleasant
aimer	to like
amusant(e)	funny
barbant(e)	boring
bien	good
bien entendu	of course
bon(ne)	good
ça dépend	it depends
ça m'énerve	it annoys me
ça me fait rire	it makes me laugh
ça me plaît	I like it
ça m'est égal	I don't care
ça ne me dit rien	it doesn't appeal to me
ça suffit	that's enough
casse-pieds	annoying
cher / chère	expensive, dear
chouette	great
comique	funny
comme ci comme ça	so-so
compliqué(e)	complicated
content(e)	pleased
croire	to believe
désagréable	unpleasant
désirer	to want
détester	to hate
difficile	difficult
dire	to say
drôle	funny
embêtant(e)	annoying
en général	in general
ennuyeux/euse	annoying, boring
espérer	to hope
étonné(e)	astonished
facile	easy
faible	weak
franchement	frankly
généralement	generally
génial(e)	great, brilliant

grave	serious
habile	skilful
incroyable	unbelievable
inquiet/iète	worried
intéressant(e)	interesting
(s') intéresser à	to be interested in
inutile	useless
joyeux/euse	joyful
marrant(e)	funny
marre (en avoir)	to be fed up
mauvais(e)	bad
merveilleux/euse	marvellous
mignon(ne)	cute
moche	ugly, rotten
moderne	modern
(moi) non plus	(me) neither
nouveau / nouvel / nouvelle	new
nul(le)	hopeless
optimiste	optimistic
passionnant(e)	exciting
penser	to think
pessimiste	pessimistic
peut-être	perhaps
populaire	popular
positif/ive	positive
pratique	practical
préférer	to prefer
promettre	to promise
regretter	to regret / be sorry
ridicule	ridiculous
rigolo(te)	funny
sage	wise, well behaved
sembler	to seem
sensass	sensational
simple	easy
splendide	splendid
stupide	stupid
superbe	superb
supporter	to put up with
utile	useful
vouloir	to want

Joyeux Noël!

C'est génial.

Ça m'énerve.

Now try this

Highlight between 10 and 15 opinion words and phrases on this page. Learn them, then see how many you can write out from memory.

1 General vocabulary

Days of the week

lundi	Monday
mardi	Tuesday
mercredi	Wednesday
jeudi	Thursday
vendredi	Friday
samedi	Saturday
dimanche	Sunday

Seasons

printemps (m)	spring
été (m)	summer
automne (m)	autumn
hiver (m)	winter

Months of the year

janvier	January
février	February
mars	March
avril	April
mai	May
juin	June
juillet	July
août	August
septembre	September
octobre	October
novembre	November
décembre	December

The clock

demi(e)	half
environ	about
heure (f)	hour
midi	midday
minuit	midnight
moins	less
quart (m)	quarter
seconde (f)	second

Other time expressions

à la fois	at the same time
à l'avenir	in the future
à l'heure	on time
à temps partiel	part-time
an (m)	year
année (f)	year
après	after
après-demain	the day after tomorrow
après-midi (m)	afternoon
aujourd'hui	today
auparavant	earlier
avant	before

avant-hier	the day before yesterday
bientôt	soon
d'abord	first
dans une minute	in a minute
d'habitude	usually
de bonne heure	early
début (m)	beginning
déjà	already
demain	tomorrow
dernier/ière	last
de temps en temps	from time to time
de nouveau	again
en attendant	meanwhile
en avance	ahead of time / early
en ce moment	at the moment
en même temps	at the same time
en retard	late
en train de (faire)	in the process of (doing)
encore une fois	once again
enfin	at last
fin (f)	end
hier	yesterday
il y a ...	... ago
jour (m)	day
journée (f)	day
lendemain (m)	the next day
longtemps	a long time
maintenant	now
matin (m)	morning
mois (m)	month
normalement	normally
nuit (f)	night
parfois	sometimes
passé (m)	past
pendant	during
plus tard	later
presque	almost
prochain(e)	next
quelquefois	sometimes
rarement	rarely
récemment	recently

semaine (f)	week
seulement	only
siècle (f)	century
soir (m)	evening
soudain	suddenly
souvent	often
suivant(e)	following
sur le point de (faire)	about to (do)
tard	late
tôt	early
toujours	always
tous les jours	every day
tout à coup	suddenly
tout de suite	immediately
vite	quickly
weekend (m)	weekend

Location and distance

à droite	on the right
à gauche	on the left
banlieue (f)	suburbs
campagne (f)	countryside
centre-ville (m)	town centre
chez (lui)	at (his) place
de chaque côté	on each side
de l'autre côté	on the other side
en bas	below
en haut	above
ici	here
là	there
là-bas	(over) there
loin de	far from
nulle part	nowhere
par	through
partout	everywhere
quelque part	somewhere
situé(e)	situated
tout droit	straight ahead
tout près	nearby
toutes directions	all routes
ville (f)	town

la France

le nord
l'ouest ✦ l'est
le sud

Now try this

Practise days and months by translating the birthdays of family and friends into French.

① General vocabulary

Colours

blanc(he)	white	
bleu(e)	blue	
brun(e)	brown	
gris(e)	grey	
jaune	yellow	
marron	brown	
noir(e)	black	
pourpre	purple	
rose	pink	
rouge	red	
vert(e)	green	

Weights and measures

boîte (f)	tin
bouteille (f)	bottle
court(e)	short
encore de	more of
étroit(e)	narrow
grand(e)	big
gros(se)	large
haut(e)	tall
large	wide
maigre	thin
mesurer	to measure
mince	slim
moitié (f)	half
morceau (m)	piece
moyen(ne)	average
nombre (m)	number
paquet (m)	packet
pas mal de	quite a few
peser	to weigh
petit(e)	small
peu	not much
plein de	lots of
pointure (f)	shoe size
rien	nothing
suffisamment	enough
taille (f)	size
tranche (f)	slice
trop	too much

Shape

carré(e)	square
hauteur (f)	height
rond(e)	round

Weather

averse (f)	shower
briller	to shine
brouillard (m)	fog
chaleur (f)	heat
chaud(e)	hot
ciel (m)	sky
climat (m)	climate
couvert(e)	overcast
degré (m)	degree
doux / douce	mild
éclair (m)	flash of lightning
éclaircie (f)	clear spell
ensoleillé(e)	sunny
il fait beau	the weather is good
il fait mauvais	the weather is bad
froid (m)	cold
geler	to freeze
glace (f)	ice
humide	humid
météo (f)	weather forecast
mouillé(e)	damp
neige (f)	snow
neiger	to snow
nuage (m)	cloud
nuageux/euse	cloudy
ombre (f)	shade
orage (m)	storm
orageux/euse	stormy
pleuvoir	to rain
pluie (f)	rain
sec / sèche	dry
soleil (m)	sun
température (f)	temperature
tempête (f)	storm
temps (m)	weather
tonnerre (f)	thunder
tremper	to soak
vent (m)	wind

Access

complet / complète	full
entrée libre	free admission
fermé(e)	closed
fermer	to close
interdit(e)	forbidden
occupé(e)	occupied
ouvert(e)	open
ouvrir	to open
sortie (f)	exit

Correctness

avoir raison	to be right
avoir tort	to be wrong
corriger	to correct
erreur (f)	mistake
faute (f)	mistake
faux / fausse	wrong
il (me) faut	I need
juste	correct
nécessaire	necessary
obligatoire	compulsory
parfait(e)	perfect
sûr(e)	sure
se tromper	to make a mistake
vrai(e)	true

Materials

argent (m)	silver
béton (m)	concrete
bois (m)	wood
brique (f)	brick
carton (m)	cardboard
coton (m)	cotton
cuir (m)	leather
fer (m)	iron
laine (f)	wool
métal (m)	metal
or (m)	gold
papier (m)	paper
plastique (m)	plastic
soie (f)	silk
verre (m)	glass

Il pleut.

Il neige.

Il y a du soleil.

Il y a du brouillard.

Il fait froid.

Il fait chaud.

Now try this

Cover up the English vocabulary in the weather list above. Highlight any words you don't know, then test yourself again in a couple of days and see how many more you know.

② Lifestyle

Health (A–P)

abricot (m)	apricot
aider	to help
alcool (m)	alcohol
alimentation (f)	food
aller bien / mieux	to be fine / better
(s') arrêter	to stop (yourself)
baguette (f)	French stick (of bread)
banane (f)	banana
beurre (m)	butter
bière (f)	beer
bifteck (m)	steak
biscuit (m)	biscuit
bœuf (m)	beef
boire	to drink
bol (m)	bowl
bonbon (m)	sweet
café (m)	café
céréales (fpl)	cereal
cerise (f)	cherry
chips (mpl)	crisps
chocolat (m) (chaud)	(hot) chocolate
chose (f)	thing
chou (m)	cabbage
chou-fleur (m)	cauliflower
cidre (m)	cider
citron (m)	lemon
coca (m)	cola
cœur (m)	heart
comprimé (m)	tablet
confiture (f)	jam
couteau (m)	knife
crème (f) (solaire)	(sun) cream
crêpe (f)	pancake
croissant (m)	croissant
cuillère (f)	spoon
cuisine (f)	kitchen
dangereux/euse	dangerous
déjeuner (m)	lunch
délicieux/ieuse	delicious
dîner (m)	evening meal
drogue (f)	drug
se droguer	to take drugs
eau (f)	water
eau minérale (f)	mineral water

eau potable / non potable (f)	drinkable / non-drinkable water
en bonne forme	in good shape
en bonne santé	in good health
envie (f) (avoir envie de)	desire (to want)
équilibré(e)	balanced
faim (f)	hunger
fatigant(e)	tiring
fatigué(e)	tired
fort(e)	strong
fourchette (f)	fork
frais / fraîche	fresh
fraise (f)	strawberry
framboise (f)	raspberry
frites (f)	chips
fromage (m)	cheese
fruits de mer (mpl)	seafood
fumer	to smoke
fumeur / non-fumeur (m)	smoking / non-smoking
gâteau (m)	cake
goût (m)	taste
goûter	to taste
gras(se)	fat, fatty
habitude (f)	habit
haricot vert (m)	green bean
hôpital (m)	hospital
hors-d'œuvre (m)	starter
huile (f)	oil
(s') inquiéter	to be worried
jambon (m)	ham
jus (m) (de fruit / d'orange)	(fruit / orange) juice
lait (m)	milk
légume (m)	vegetable
limonade (f)	lemonade
liste (f)	list
mal (m) (avoir mal)	hurt (to hurt)
malade	ill
maladie (f)	illness
manger	to eat
médecin (m)	doctor
médicament (m)	drug, medication
nourriture (f)	food
obésité (f)	obesity
odeur (f)	smell

œuf (m)	egg
ordinaire	ordinary
pain (m)	bread
paresseux/euse	lazy
pâté (m)	pâté
pâtes (fpl)	pasta
pêche (f)	peach
petit déjeuner (m)	breakfast
peur (f)	fear
plein(e)	full
poire (f)	pear
poisson (m)	fish
poivre (m)	pepper
pomme (f)	apple
porc (m)	pork
poulet (m)	chicken
prendre	to take

carotte (f)

champignon (m)

oignon (m)

petits pois (m/pl)

poivron (m)

pomme de terre (f)

tomate (f)

citron (m)

pomme (f)

ananas (m)

Now try this

To help you learn the food words, write out the French words in two lists: foods that are healthy and foods that are unhealthy. Then memorise five foods that you like and five foods that you dislike.

② Lifestyle

Health (Q–Z)

raisin (m)	grape(s)
régime (m)	diet
(se) relaxer	to relax
repas (m)	meal
rester	to stay
riz (m)	rice
rôti(e)	roast
sain(e)	healthy
salade (f)	salad
sans	without
santé (f)	health
saucisse (f)	sausage
saucisson (m) (sec)	(dried) sausage
sauf	except
saumon (m)	salmon
sel (m)	salt
(se) sentir	to feel
soif (f)	thirst
soupe (f)	soup
spaghettis (mpl)	spaghetti
spécialité (f)	speciality
sucré(e)	sweet
sucre (m)	sugar
surtout	especially
tabac (m)	tobacco
tarte (f)	tart
thé (m)	tea
tomber	to fall
tousser	to cough
truite (f)	trout
vanille (f)	vanilla
végétarien(ne)	vegetarian
verre (m)	glass
viande (f)	meat
vide	empty
vin (m)	wine
vitamine (f)	vitamin
vivre	to live
yaourt (m)	yoghurt

Health

à la carte	à la carte (menu)
à peine	scarcely
à point	medium (cooked, of meat)
accro	addicted
activité physique (f)	physical activity
agneau (m)	lamb
ail (m)	garlic
alcoolique	alcoholic
alcoolisé(e)	alcoholic
alcoolisme (m)	alcoholism
alimentation saine (f)	healthy food
amer / amère	bitter
ananas (m)	pineapple
apéritif (m)	aperitif
avertir	to warn
bien cuit(e)	well cooked
canard (m)	duck
casse-croûte (m)	snack
casserole (f)	(sauce)pan
concombre (m)	cucumber
côtelette (f)	cutlet
crevette (f)	prawn
crise cardiaque (f)	heart attack
cru(e)	raw
crudités (fpl)	raw vegetables
dégoûtant(e)	disgusting
dégustation (f)	tasting
désintoxiquer	to detox
(se) détendre	to relax
douleur (f)	pain
(s') entraîner	to train
épais(se)	thick

épicé(e)	spicy
épuiser	to exhaust
escargot (m)	snail
faire la grasse matinée	to have a lie-in
farine (f)	flour
foie (m)	liver
gâcher	to waste, to spoil
hors d'haleine	out of breath
huître (f)	oyster
ivre	drunk
laitue (f)	lettuce
matières grasses (fpl)	fats
mener	to lead
noix (f)	walnut
ouvre-boîte (m)	tin opener
pamplemousse (m)	grapefruit
piquant(e)	hot (spicy)
piqûre (f)	sting, injection
poumon (m)	lung
prune (f)	plum
renoncer	to give up
reprendre connaissance	to regain consciousness
respirer	to breathe
revendeur (m)	dealer
saignant(e)	bleeding, rare
salé(e)	salted
sauvegarder	to save
savoureux/euse	tasty
sommeil (m) (avoir sommeil)	sleep (to be sleepy)
tabagisme (m)	smoking
tire-bouchon (m)	corkscrew
toxicomane (m/f)	drug addict
tuer	to kill
veau (m)	veal
veine (f)	vein
vinaigre (m)	vinegar
voler	to steal

alimentation saine (f)

un jus de fruit

une salade verte

Now try this

Make a list in French of between 10 and 15 words on this page connected with health issues. Close the book and try to write the English. Check back to see how many you got right.

2 Lifestyle

Relationships and choices

adresse (f)	address
adulte (m/f)	adult
âge (m)	age
aimable	kind
aîné(e)	eldest
ami(e) (m/f)	friend
amical(e)	friendly
amour (m)	love
anniversaire (m)	birthday
annonce (f)	announcement
(s') appeler	to be called
attendre	to wait
avoir... ans	to be... years old
barbe (f)	beard
battre	to beat
bavard(e)	talkative
bavarder	to chat
beau / belle	beautiful
beau-frère (m)	stepbrother, brother-in-law
beau-père (m)	stepfather, father-in-law
bébé (m)	baby
belle-mère (f)	stepmother, mother-in-law
belle-sœur (f)	stepsister, sister-in-law
bête	stupid
bouclé(e)	curly
carte d'identité (f)	identity card
célèbre	famous
cher / chère	dear
cheval (m)	horse
cheveux (mpl)	hair
chômage (m)	unemployment
connaître	to know (person)
contribuer	to contribute
copain (m)	(boy)friend
copine (f)	(girl)friend
critiquer	to criticise
dame (f)	woman
date de naissance (f)	date of birth
demi-frère (m)	half-brother
demi-sœur (f)	half-sister
(se) disputer	to argue
divorcé(e)	divorced
écrire	to write

égoïste	selfish
enfant (m/f)	child
(s') entendre	to get along
fâché(e)	annoyed
famille (f)	family
femme (f)	woman, wife
fille (f)	girl, daughter
fils (m)	son
frère (m)	brother
garçon (m)	boy
gens (mpl)	people
gentil(le)	nice
grand-mère (f)	grandmother
grand-père (m)	grandfather
grands-parents (mpl)	grandparents
(s') habituer à	to get used to
hésiter	to hesitate
heureux/euse	happy
homme (m)	man
il s'agit de	it's about
jeune	young
joli(e)	pretty
lieu (m)	place
loger	to stay
lunettes (fpl) (de soleil)	(sun)glasses
malheureux/euse	unhappy
mari (m)	husband
marié(e)	married
(se) marier	to get married
méchant(e)	naughty
mère (f)	mother
mort (f)	death
naissance (f)	birth
nationalité (f)	nationality
né(e)	born
nez (m)	nose
nom (m) (de famille)	(sur)name
oiseau (m)	bird
oncle (m)	uncle
parents (m)	parents
partenaire (m/f) (idéal(e))	(ideal) partner
passeport (m)	passport
pauvre	poor
pénible	difficult
père (m)	father
personnalité (f)	personality
personne (f)	person
personnes défavorisées (fpl)	disadvantaged people
petit ami (m)	boyfriend
petite amie (f)	girlfriend
pleurer	to cry
poli(e)	polite
porter	to wear

prénom (m)	first name
rapports (mpl)	relations
refuser	to refuse
religieux/ieuse	religious
remercier	to thank
rendez-vous (m)	date
respecter	to respect
responsabilité (f)	responsibility
riche	rich
rire	to laugh
sans travail	unemployed
sécurité (f)	security
sens de l'humour (m)	sense of humour
séparé(e)	separated
seul(e)	alone
signer	to sign
sœur (f)	sister
sondage (m)	survey
sourire	to smile
souris (f)	mouse
sympa	nice, friendly
tante (f)	aunt
timide	shy
tranquille	quiet
triste	sad
vandalisme (m)	vandalism
vérité (f)	truth
vieux / vieille	old
visage (m)	face
voisin(e) (m/f)	neighbour

chat (m)

chien (m)

cochon d'Inde (m)

lapin (m)

poisson rouge (m)

poisson tropical (m)

Now try this

To help you learn the personality adjectives, write out the French words in three lists: positive, negative and neutral. Then memorise five adjectives that could describe you.

② Lifestyle

Relationships and choices

actif/ive	active
ado (m/f)	adolescent
agresser	to attack
alliance (f)	marriage
animé(e)	lively
attaque (f)	attack
bague (f)	ring
baiser (m)	kiss
bande (f)	gang
bonheur (f)	happiness
brutaliser	to ill-treat
cacher	to hide
caractère (m)	character
célibataire	single
chrétien(ne)	Christian
compréhensif/ive	understanding
compter sur	to depend on
consacrer	to dedicate
conseil (m)	piece of advice
coupable (m)	guilty party
de mauvaise humeur	in a bad mood
(se) débrouiller	to cope
déçu(e)	disappointed
déprimé(e)	depressed
déranger	to disturb
dette (f)	debt
douter	to doubt
droits de l'homme (mpl)	human rights
effrayant(e)	frightening
égal(e)	equal
égalité (f)	equality
élégant(e)	elegant
enlèvement (m)	kidnap

ennui (m)	boredom, problem
enquête (f)	inquiry
envahir	to invade
épouser	to marry
espoir (m)	hope
esprit (m)	mind
étonnant(e)	astonishing
étrange	strange
éviter	to avoid
exclus (m/fpl)	outcasts
exprès	deliberately
féliciter	to congratulate
fêter	to celebrate
fiançailles (fpl)	engagement
fiancé(e) (m/f)	fiancé(e)
fier / fière	proud
fou / folle	mad
gâter	to spoil
gêner	to embarrass
humilier	to humiliate
illégal(e)	illegal
immigré(e) (m/f)	immigrant
inconnu(e)	unknown
jaloux / jalouse	jealous
jeunesse (f)	youth
jugement (m)	judgement
juif / juive	Jewish
jumeau (m)	twin (male)
jumelle (f)	twin (female)
laid(e)	ugly
libertés civiques (fpl)	civil liberties
lutter	to fight
maigre	thin
maladroit(e)	awkward
manifestation (f)	demonstration
menacer	to threaten
(se) mettre en colère	to get angry
monoparental(e)	single-parent
moral (m)	moral

mosquée (f)	mosque
mourir	to die
musulman(e)	Muslim
naître	to be born
nerveux/euse	nervous
neveu (m)	nephew
nièce (f)	niece
noces (fpl)	wedding
nostalgie (f)	nostalgia
organisation caritative (f)	charitable organisation
pauvreté (f)	poverty
petite-fille (f)	granddaughter
petit-fils (m)	grandson
(se) plaindre	to complain
plaire	to please
plaisir (m)	pleasure
racaille (f)	riffraff
racisme (m)	racism
raide	stoned
réaliser	to carry out
reconnaissant(e)	grateful
réfléchir	to reflect
réfugié(e) (m/f)	refugee
retraite (f)	retirement
(à la retraite)	(retired)
rêver	to dream
sans ressources	poor
sans-abri (m/fpl)	homeless
sentiment (m)	feeling
(se) séparer	to separate
sida (m)	Aids
surveiller	to supervise
témoin (m)	witness
tomber amoureux de	to fall in love with
travail bénévole	voluntary work (m)
veuf (m)	widower
veuve (f)	widow
vif / vive	lively
vol (m)	theft
voyou (m)	lout

épouser

une manifestation

la pauvreté

Now try this

Draw your family tree and label it in French or make a list in French of your relatives. Use this page to check that your spelling is accurate.

③ Leisure

Free time and the media (A–I)

accompagner	to accompany
achat (m)	purchase
acheter	to buy
aller	to go
(s') amuser	to have a good time
à l'appareil (m)	speaking (on phone)
appel (m)	call
argent (m) (de poche)	(pocket) money
avantage (m)	advantage
ballon (m)	ball
bande dessinée (f)	cartoon
banque (f)	bank
basket (m)	basketball
besoin (m) (avoir... de)	need (to need)
bijouterie (f)	jewellery
billet (m)	ticket
blouson (m)	jacket
bon marché	cheap
boucherie (f)	butcher's
boucle d'oreille (f)	earring
boulangerie (f)	baker's
boules (fpl)	bowls
boutique (f)	shop
cadeau (m)	present
caisse (f)	checkout
carte de crédit (f)	credit card
ceinture (f)	belt
centre commercial (m)	shopping centre
centre de sport (m)	sports centre
chanson (f)	song
chanter	to sing
chanteur (m)	singer
chanteuse (f)	singer
charcuterie (f)	delicatessen
chaussure (f)	shoe
chemise (f)	shirt
choisir	to choose
choix (m)	choice

cinéma (m)	cinema
clavier (m)	keyboard
client (m)	client
cliquer	to click
coiffeur (m)	hairdresser
coiffeuse (f)	hairdresser
coin (m)	corner
comédie (f)	comedy
concours (m)	competition
confiserie (f)	confectioner's
couleur (f)	colour
courir	to run
cyclisme (m)	cycling
danser	to dance
démodé(e)	old-fashioned
dépenser	to spend
désavantage (m)	disadvantage
dessin animé (m)	cartoon
documentaire (m)	documentary
donner	to give
échanger	to exchange
écran (m)	screen
émission (f) (jeunesse / musicale / sportive)	programme (youth / music / sports)
ensemble	together
entrée (f)	admission, ticket
envoyer	to send
épicerie (f)	grocer's
équipe (f)	team
équitation (f)	horse-riding
essayer	to try
faire des économies	to save
faire les courses	to go shopping
faire les magasins	to go shopping
fana (m/f) (être fana de)	fan (to be a fan of)
favori / favorite	favourite
feuilleton (m)	serial, soap opera
film d'aventures (m)	adventure film
film d'horreur (m)	horror film
film de guerre (m)	war film
film de science-fiction (m)	science fiction film
film policier (m)	detective film
film romantique (m)	romantic film

gagner	to win
gant (m)	glove
gratuit(e)	free
groupe (m)	group
guitare (f)	guitar
gymnastique (f)	gymnastics
hypermarché (m)	hypermarket
idée (f)	idea
imper(méable) (m)	raincoat
inconvénient (m)	disadvantage

 chaussette (f)

 chaussure (f)

 ceinture (f)

 chapeau (m)

 écharpe (f)

 cravate (f)

 chemise (f)

 jupe (f)

Now try this

Look at the clothes that you and your friends are wearing today. Check that you can write and say them all in French.

③ Leisure

Free time and the media (J–S)

jean (m) — jeans
jeu (m) (de cartes / de société) — (card / board) game
jeu vidéo (m) — video game
jouer — to play
jouet (m) — toy
journal (m) — newspaper
jupe (f) — skirt
laisser — to leave, to let
lecteur DVD (m) — DVD player
lecteur MP3 (m) — MP3 player
lecture (f) — reading
librairie (f) — bookshop
lire — to read
livre sterling (f) — pound sterling
magasin (m) — shop
maillot de bain (m) — swimsuit
maison de la presse (f) — newsagent's
manteau (m) — coat
maquillage (m) — make-up
marchand (m) (de fruits et de légumes) — (fruit and vegetable) shopkeeper
marché (m) — market
membre (m) — member
mettre de l'argent à côté — to save money
mode (f) (à la mode) — fashion (fashionable)
monnaie (f) — change (money)
montre (f) — watch
musique (f) (classique / pop / rap / rock) — music (classical / pop / rap / rock)

nager — to swim
natation (f) — swimming
numéro (m) (de téléphone) — (telephone) number
orchestre (m) — orchestra
ordinateur (m) — computer
paire (f) — pair
pantalon (m) — trousers
parapluie (m) — umbrella
parfum (m) — perfume
parfumerie (f) — perfume shop
passe-temps (m) — pastime
patin à roulettes (m) — roller skating
patinage (m) — skating
patiner — to skate
patinoire (f) — skating rink
pâtisserie (f) — cake shop
pêche (f) — fishing
pièce (f) — play
pique-nique (m) — picnic
piscine (f) — swimming pool
planche à voile (f) — surfing
poche (f) — pocket
portable (m) — (mobile) phone
portefeuille (m) — wallet
porte-monnaie (m) — purse
poste (f) — post office
pousser — to push
prix (m) — price
(se) promener — to go for a walk
publicité (f) — advertisement
pull (m) — pullover
pyjama (m) — pyjamas
rayon (m) — department
recevoir — to receive
réduction (f) — reduction
réduit(e) — reduced

regarder — to look at
remplir — to fill
(se) rencontrer — to meet
rentrer — to go home
retourner — to return
risque (m) — risk
robe (f) — dress
rouge à lèvres (m) — lipstick
sac (m) (à main) — (hand)bag
sandale (f) — sandal
sauter — to jump
séance (f) — performance
série (f) — series
shampooing (m) — shampoo
short (m) — shorts
site (m) (aller sur un site) — website (to go onto a website)
skate (m) — skateboarding
ski nautique (m) — water-skiing
soldes (mpl) — sale
sortie (f) — exit, excursion
sortir — to go out
sous-titré(e) — subtitled
spectateur (m) — spectator
sportif / sportive — sporty
sports d'hiver (mpl) — winter sports
sports nautiques (mpl) — water sports
stade (m) — stadium
supermarché (m) — supermarket
surf (m) (de neige) — snowboarding
surfer — to surf
surprise-partie (f) — party
sweat (shirt) (m) — sweatshirt

jouer au basket

jouer au tennis

faire du vélo

faire de la danse

faire de l'équitation

faire de l'escalade

faire de la gymnastique

faire du patin à roulettes

Now try this

Make a list of five sports on this page that you have tried and five that you have not tried. Then memorise them.

③ Leisure

Free time and the media (T–Z)

taper	to key / type in
technologie (f)	technology
télé(vision) (f)	television
temps libre (m)	free time
texto (m)	SMS
théâtre (m)	theatre
tirer	to pull
toucher	to touch
valeur (f)	value
vedette (f)	(film) star
vendre	to sell
venir	to come
version (f) (originale / française)	(original / French) version
veste (f)	jacket
vêtements (mpl)	clothes
vitrine (f)	shop window
voile (f)	sailing
voir	to see
volley (m)	volleyball
VTT (m)	mountain-biking

Free time and the media

actualités (fpl)	news
alpinisme (m)	mountaineering
annuler	to cancel
anonyme	anonymous
antenne (f)	aerial
bijou (m)	jewel
bloggeur (m)	blogger
boîte (f) aux lettres électronique (blé)	(email) inbox
bouton (m)	button
caméscope (m)	camcorder
canoë-kayak (m)	canoeing
chaîne (f)	channel
chariot (m)	trolley
chemisier (m)	blouse
commencement (m)	beginning

commerçant(e) (m/f)	trader
comptoir (m)	counter
console de jeu (f)	games console
contrôler	to check
courrier électronique (m)	email
course (f)	running
cybercafé (m)	internet café
déchirer	to tear (up)
dérouler (en bas / en haut)	to scroll (down / up)
deviner	to guess
distractions (fpl)	entertainment
distributeur automatique (m)	vending machine
échecs (m)	chess
écran tactile (m)	touchscreen
effacer	to erase
emballer	to wrap
emprunter	to borrow
(s') ennuyer	to be bored
enregistrer	to record
escalade (f)	climbing
être remboursé(e)	to be refunded
événement (m)	event
faire du lèche-vitrines	to go window-shopping
fermeture (f) (annuelle)	(annual) closure
feu d'artifice (m)	firework display
feuilleter	to flip through
fléchettes (fpl)	darts
fleuriste (m/f)	florist
genre (m)	kind, sort
grande surface (f)	superstore
grille de sécurité (f)	security grid
gymnase (m)	gymnasium
icône (f)	icon
imprimer	to print out
jour férié (m)	(public) holiday
lancer	to run (program)
libre-service (m)	self-service
lien (m)	link
lourd(e)	heavy
magnétoscope (m)	video recorder

marquer (un but)	to score (a goal)
mettre en ligne	to put online
mi-temps (f)	half-time
moniteur (m)	monitor (computer)
mots croisés (mpl)	crossword
musculation (f) (faire de la musculation)	body-building (to do weight-training)
page d'accueil (f)	home page
pédagogique	educational
piercing (m) (à l'oreille)	(ear) piercing
pile (f)	battery
planche de surf (f)	surfboard
platine laser (f)	CD player
plongée sous-marine (f)	scuba diving
poissonnerie (f)	fishmonger's
poste de travail (m)	workstation
prise (f)	socket
pull à capuche (m)	hoodie
quotidien(ne)	daily
réclame (f) (en réclame)	advertisement (for sale)
reçu (m)	receipt
rembourser	to refund
remplacer	to replace
remporter (un prix)	to win (a prize)
réseau (m)	network
reste (m)	remainder
réunion (f)	meeting
sommet (m)	summit
suggérer	to suggest
tatouage (m)	tattoo
télécharger	to download, to upload
téléspectateur (m)	(TV) viewer
tournée (f)	tour, round
traitement de texte (m)	word processing

écouter de la musique

jouer aux échecs

lire

faire de la voile

faire de l'escalade

Now try this

Make a list of all the free time activities on these two pages, under three headings:
- Those you like
- Those you don't like
- Those you feel neutral about.

4 Home and environment

Home and local area

appartement (m)	apartment
arbre (m)	tree
armoire (f)	wardrobe
arrêt (m) (d'autobus)	bus stop
(s') asseoir	to sit down
bâtiment (m)	building
bibliothèque (f)	library
boîte de nuit (f)	nightclub
boum (f)	party
bowling (m)	bowling alley
bruit (m)	noise
bureau (m)	office
calme	quiet
cathédrale (f)	cathedral
cave (f)	cellar
chaise (f)	chair
champ (m)	field
clé (f)	key
club des jeunes (m)	youth club
code postal (m)	postcode
colline (f)	hill
commissariat (m)	police station
confortable	comfortable
(se) coucher	to go to bed
couloir (m)	passage, hall
cuisinière (f)	cooker
déménager	to move home
descendre	to go down
dormir	to sleep
église (f)	church
entrer	to go in
escalier (m)	stairs
espace (m)	space
étage (m)	floor
faire du baby-sitting	to babysit
faire du jardinage	to garden
faire le ménage	to do the housework
faire la vaisselle	to do the dishes
fenêtre (f)	window
ferme (f)	farm
fête (f)	festival, party
feu (m)	fire

fleur (f)	flower
four (m) (à micro-ondes)	(microwave) oven
frigo (m)	fridge
garder	to keep
habitant(e) (m/f)	inhabitant
habiter	to live
historique	historic
hôtel de ville (m)	town hall
île (f)	island
immeuble (m)	building, block of flats
industrie (f)	industry
industriel(le)	industrial
jardin (m)	garden
jardin publique (m)	park
lampe (f)	lamp
lave-vaisselle (m)	dishwasher
(se) laver	to wash (yourself)
laver la voiture	to wash the car
se lever	to get up
lit (m)	bed
mairie (f)	town hall
maison (f) (individuelle / jumelée)	(detached / semi-detached) house
mariage (m)	marriage
métro (m)	underground
mettre	to put
meuble (m)	piece of furniture
miroir (m)	mirror
montagne (f)	mountain
monter	to go up
montrer	to show
mur (m)	wall
musée (m)	museum
nettoyer	to clean
Noël	Christmas
Nouvel An (m)	New Year

Pâques	Easter
parc (m)	park
parking (m)	car park
pelouse (f)	lawn
pièce (f)	room
placard (m)	cupboard
place (f)	square
plafond (m)	ceiling
plante (f)	plant
pont (m)	bridge
porte (f) (d'entrée)	(front) door
privé(e)	private
quartier (m)	district
réveil (m)	alarm clock
(se) réveiller	to wake up
rez-de-chaussée (m)	ground floor
rideau (m)	curtain
rivière (f)	river
Saint-Valentin (f)	Valentine's Day
salle à manger (f)	dining room
salle de séjour (f)	living room
salon (m)	lounge
serviette (f)	towel
sous-sol (m)	basement
tableau (m)	painting
tapis (m)	carpet
téléphone (m)	phone
téléphoner	to phone
terrain (m) (de camping / de sport)	(camping / sports) ground
terrasse (f)	terrace
toit (m)	roof
trottoir (m)	pavement
(se) trouver	to be situated
usine (f)	factory
vache (f)	cow
vestibule (m)	hall
vie (f)	life

une cathédrale

un château

une église

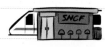
une gare SNCF

un hôtel de ville / une mairie

un jardin zoologique

un musée

une plage

Now try this

Make a list in French of all the amenities your local town has, and a list of the amenities it doesn't have. Test yourself on the French spellings.

④ Home and environment

Home and local area

allumer	to switch on
appuyer	to support
arrondissement (m)	district
baptême (m)	baptism
bricolage (m)	DIY
bruyant(e)	noisy
concierge (m/f)	caretaker
couverture (f)	cover
couvrir	to cover
donner sur	to overlook
dur(e)	hard
échelle (f)	ladder
entouré(e)	surrounded
espaces verts (mpl)	green / open spaces
étagère (f)	shelves
éteindre	to put out, to turn off
fauteuil (m)	armchair
feuille (f)	leaf
fontaine (f)	fountain
forêt (f)	forest
grenier (m)	attic
haie (f)	hedge
herbe (f)	grass
horloge (f)	clock
inondation (f)	flood
jardin zoologique (m)	zoo
jour de l'an (m)	New Year's Day
jumelé(e)	twinned
lits superposés (mpl)	bunk beds
moquette (f)	carpet
palais (m)	palace
pittoresque	picturesque

ranger	to tidy
robinet (m)	tap
Saint-Sylvestre (f)	New Year's Eve
sans intérêt	uninteresting
spacieux/ieuse	spacious
terre (f)	earth
tiroir (m)	drawer
Toussaint (f)	Halloween
volet (m)	shutter

Environment

boîte (f) (en carton)	(cardboard) box
centre de recyclage (m)	recycling centre
circulation (f)	traffic
cultiver	to grow
déchets (mpl)	waste
environnement (m)	environment
jeter	to throw away
pétrole (m)	oil
piste cyclable (f)	cycle lane
pollué(e)	polluted
poubelle (f)	waste bin
problème (m)	problem
propre	clean
protéger	to protect
recyclable	recyclable
recycler	to recycle
sac en plastique (m)	plastic bag
sale	dirty
sans plomb	lead-free
sauver	to save
transports en commun (mpl)	public transport
zone (f) (piétonne)	(pedestrian) area

Environment

augmenter	to increase
charbon (m)	coal
consommation (f) (modérée)	(moderate) consumption
construire	to build
couche d'ozone (f)	ozone layer
croire	to believe
déboisement (m)	deforestation
détritus (mpl)	rubbish
détruire	to destroy
disparaître	to disappear
effet de serre (m)	greenhouse effect
emballage (m)	packaging
embouteillage (m)	traffic jam
endommager	to damage
espèce (f)	species
gaz carbonique (m)	carbon dioxide
gaz d'échappement (m)	exhaust fumes
guerre (f)	war
heures d'affluence (fpl)	rush hour
incendie (m)	fire
lumière (f)	light
mondial(e)	world, global
ordures (fpl)	rubbish
paix (f)	peace
produire	to produce
ramasser	to pick up
réchauffement de la terre (m)	global warming
renouvelable	renewable
surpeuplé(e)	overpopulated
tremblement de terre (m)	earthquake
trou d'ozone (m)	hole in the ozone layer
vague (f)	wave

Il y a des fontaines.

Nous utilisons trop d'emballages.

Now try this

Highlight between 10 and 15 words on this page that you may use when talking about the environment. Learn them, then write out the ones you find difficult to remember.

⑤ Work and education

School / college and future plans (A–P)

affaires (fpl)	personal belongings
apprendre	to learn
apprenti(e) (m/f)	apprentice
apprentissage (m)	apprenticeship
arts ménagers (mpl)	cookery, food technology
bac(calauréat) (m)	equivalent of A levels
biologie (f)	biology
brevet (m)	GCSE equivalent
cahier (m)	exercise book
calculatrice (f)	calculator
carrière (f)	career
chimie (f)	chemistry
collège (m)	(secondary) school
commencer	to begin
commerce (m)	business studies
comprendre	to understand
copier	to copy
cour (f)	(school) yard
cours (m)	lesson
crayon (m)	pencil
défense de...	... is forbidden
demander	to ask
dessin (m)	drawing
dessiner	to draw
détail (m)	detail
détester	to hate

devoir	to have to
devoirs (mpl)	homework
dictionnaire (m)	dictionary
difficile	difficult
difficulté (f)	difficulty
directeur (m)	head teacher
directrice (f)	head teacher
discuter	to discuss
droit (m)	right
échange (m)	exchange
école (f) (primaire / secondaire)	(primary / secondary) school
économie (f)	economics
écouter	to listen
élève (m/f)	pupil
emploi du temps (m)	timetable
EMT: éducation manuelle et technique	DT
en première	in year 12
en quatrième	in year 9
en seconde	in year 11
en sixième	in year 7
en terminale	in year 13
en troisième	in year 10
encourager	to encourage
EPS: éducation physique et sportive	technology
espagnol (m)	Spanish
études (fpl) (des médias)	(media) studies
étudiant(e) (m/f)	student
étudier	to study
examen (m)	exam
exemple (m)	example

facile	easy
faire attention	to pay attention
finir	to finish
français (m)	French
géographie (f)	geography
histoire (f)	history
informatique (f)	IT
inquiet / iète	worried
instituteur (m)	(primary school) teacher
institutrice (f)	(primary school) teacher
instruction civique (f)	PSHCE
instruction religieuse (f)	religion, RE
italien (f)	Italian
laboratoire (m)	lab
langue (f)	language
langues étrangères (fpl)	modern languages
langues vivantes (fpl)	modern languages
leçon (f)	lesson
livre (m)	book
lycée (f) (technique)	(technical) college
math(s) (fpl)	maths
mathématiques (fpl)	mathematics
matière (f)	subject
mot (m)	word
note (f)	mark
organiser	to organise
oublier	to forget
parler	to speak
passer	to take (an exam)

 l'allemand (m)

 l'anglais (m)

 le dessin

l'espagnol (m)

 le français

 la biologie

 la chimie

la physique

$y^2+2=x$ les mathématiques / maths (fpl)

 l'informatique (f)

 la géographie

 l'histoire (f)

 l'instruction religieuse (f)

 l'EPS / éducation physique (f)

Now try this

What GCSEs are you and your friends taking? Check that you can say and write them all in French. If you're thinking of doing some subjects at A level, can you translate those too?

⑤ Work and education

School / college and future plans (P–Z)

pause (f)	break
penser	to think
perdre	to lose
photocopie (f)	photocopy
physique (f)	physics
poser	to ask
pouvoir	to be able
préparer	to prepare for (an exam)
professeur (m)	(secondary school) teacher
récréation (f)	break
règle (f)	rule, ruler
règlement (m)	rules
rentrée (f)	back to school
répéter	to repeat
répondre	to answer
réponse (f)	answer
résultat (m)	result
réviser	to revise
salle de classe (f)	classroom
savoir	to know
sciences (fpl)	sciences
scolaire	academic, school
sociologie (f)	sociology
stylo (m)	pen
tableau (m) (blanc interactif)	(interactive white)board
technologie (f)	technology
travailler	to work
travailleur/euse	hard-working
trimestre (m)	term
uniforme (m)	uniform
université (f)	university
utiliser	to use
vocabulaire (m)	vocabulary

School / college and future plans

bien équipé(e)	well equipped
car de ramassage (m)	school bus
confiance (f)	confidence
connaissance (f)	knowledge
couramment	fluently
diplôme (m)	diploma

doué(e)	gifted, talented
échouer	to fail
empêcher	to prevent
enseigner	to teach
enthousiasme (m)	enthusiasm
explication (f)	explanation
faculté (f)	faculty, department
frapper	to impress, to strike
incivilités (mpl)	bad behaviour
licence (f)	degree
mal équipé(e)	badly equipped
maternelle (f)	nursery school
mentir	to lie
permettre	to allow
progrès (mpl)	progress
redoubler	to repeat a year
retenue (f)	detention
réussir	to succeed
salle d'informatique (f)	IT room
salle des professeurs (f)	staffroom
souci (m)	worry, care
surchargé(e)	overloaded
tâche (f)	task
(se) taire	to be quiet
thème (m)	theme, translation (into another language)
traduire	to translate
troisième âge (m)	older, third age
utiliser	to use
victime (f)	victim

Current and future jobs (A–C)

acteur (m)	actor
actrice (f)	actress
avenir (m)	future
bien payé(e)	well paid
boîte aux lettres (f)	letter/post box
boucher (m)	butcher
boulanger (m)	baker
boulot (m)	job
caissier (m)	cashier
candidat (m)	candidate

certainement	certainly
certificat (m)	certificate
chef (m)	boss, chef
collègue (m/f)	colleague, co-worker
conférence (f)	conference, meeting

Current and future jobs (D–Z)

décider	to decide
devenir	to become
distribuer	to distribute
docteur (m)	doctor
électricien (m)	electrician
emploi (m)	job, employment
entreprise (f)	business, company
enveloppe (f)	envelope
épicier (m)	grocer
facteur (m)	postman
fermier (m)	farmer
formulaire (m)	form
hôtesse de l'air (f)	air stewardess
infirmier (m)	nurse
infirmière (f)	nurse
ingénieur (m)	engineer
lettre (f)	letter
livrer	to deliver
mal payé(e)	badly paid
mécanicien (m)	mechanic
musicien (m)	musician
paquet (m)	packet, parcel
patron (m)	boss
plombier (m)	plumber
policier (m)	police officer
programmeur (m)	programmer
propriétaire (m/f)	owner
(se) rappeler	to remember
rêve (m)	dream
salaire (m)	salary
secrétaire (m/f)	secretary
serveur (m)	waiter
serveuse (f)	waitress
stage (m) (en entreprise)	training (in a business)
technicien (m)	technician
timbre (m)	stamp
travail (m)	work
varié(e)	varied
vendeur (m)	salesman
vendeuse (f)	saleswoman

Now try this

Pick five verbs on this page and write each of them out with *je*, in the future tense.

⑤ Work and education

Current and future jobs

améliorer	to improve
annuaire (m)	directory
assurer	to make sure of, to insure
auteur (m)	author
avertissement (m)	warning
avocat (m)	lawyer
cadre (m)	executive (in business)
comptable (m)	accountant
contrat (m)	contract
cours professionnel (m)	vocational course, in-service training
demande d'emploi (f)	job application
écrivain (m)	writer
enrichissant(e)	rewarding, enriching
entretien (m)	interview
épreuve (f)	test
femme de ménage (f)	housekeeper, cleaner
foire d'exposition (f)	(trade) faire, exhibition
homme au foyer (m)	house-husband
informaticien (m)	computer scientist
interprète (m/f)	interpreter
jardinier (m)	gardener
licencier	to dismiss
loi (f)	law
maçon (m)	bricklayer
mannequin (m)	model
offre d'emploi (f)	job offer
ouvrier (m)	(manual) worker
programme de formation (m)	training programme
soigner	to look after, to take care of
soin (m)	care
vétérinaire (m/f)	vet

 un(e) avocat(e)

 un(e) caissier / caissière

 un(e) comptable

 un(e) électricien(ne)

 un(e) facteur / factrice

 un(e) fermier / fermière

 un(e) informaticien(ne)

 un(e) maçon(ne)

 un(e) médecin / docteur

 un(e) policier / policière

 un(e) serveur / serveuse

 un(e) vétérinaire

New vocabulary

Now try this

To help you learn the jobs vocabulary, make a list of five jobs that you would like to do and five that you would not like to do. Then memorise them.

Answers

Lifestyle

1. Birthdays
1 Name: Benjamin
  Age: 16
  Birthday: 21st December
2 Name: Adrien
  Age: 17
  Birthday: 30th March
3 Name: Francine
  Age: 19
  Birthday: 1st July
4 Name: Yasmine
  Age: 13
  Birthday: 23rd June

2. Pets
(a) L (b) M (c) J (d) T

4. Personality
A, D, E, G

6. Family
(a) T (b) ? (c) F (d) T

8. Daily routine
1 C 2 A 3 B 4 C

11. Eating in a café
Olivier: B   Adèle: B

12. Eating in a restaurant
(a) N (b) C (c) M (d) N

13. Healthy eating
(a) F (b) C (c) A (d) A

15. Health problems
(a) F (b) F (c) G (d) A

17. Social issues
1 C 2 D

18. Social problems
(a) P/N (b) N (c) P

Leisure

20. Sport
(a) T (b) F (c) T (d) F
(e) T (f) F

21. Going out
(a) the swimming pool
(b) do homework
(c) the leisure centre
(d) walk the dog

22. Last weekend
(a) nice and hot
(b) have a picnic, swim
(c) she broke her leg
(d) It wasn't boring at all. Her friends came round. / She watched a DVD and ate pizza with her friends.

24. Cinema
A, B, F

26. New technology
1 receives texts
2 watches films
3 plays games
4 takes photos

27. Internet language
(b) *two of:* simple, effective, free

29. Shops
1 E 2 C 3 D 4 B 5 A

30. Food shopping
(a) a packet
(b) peaches
(c) four slices
(d) 200 g
(e) strawberry yoghurts
(f) three pieces

31. Shopping
(a) connect your MP3 player to the receiver
(b) in your pocket or your bag
(c) within 12 metres

32. Clothes
1 C, 3 2 A, 1 3 D, 6 4 E, 4

36. Pocket money
Amélie: E, C   Raoul: F, B

37. Holiday destinations
(a) C (b) M (c) R
(d) M (e) C

39. Booking accommodation
1 A 2 C 3 A

40. Staying in a hotel
(a) the south of France / a small family hotel by the beach
(b) *one of:* swimming pool / games room
   one of: air conditioning / lift
(c) *two of:* still being built / they couldn't see the sea / they couldn't sleep because of the noise / there was nothing for the children to do / the air conditioning didn't work
(d) that they would never go back to that hotel

42. Holiday activities
1 C 2 D 3 A 4 G

45. Holiday experiences
(a) his best friend (Brice)
(b) it was for 13–17 year olds
(c) they stayed in a very large chalet; they shared their room with two other boys
(d) they were very hungry after a day skiing

Home and environment

47. My house

	Type of house / flat	Doesn't have
Hugo:	flat in large block	dining room

49. Helping at home
1 N 2 P/N 3 P

50. Where I live
2 attirent 3 trottoirs
4 pour 5 rêve
6 être 7 serait

52. Things to do in town
1 F 2 E 3 B 4 A

54. Signs around town
(a) bakery
(b) in advance
(c) Sunday

56. Town description
1 C 2 B 3 A

57. Weather
(a) T (b) F (c) T (d) F
(e) ? (f) T (g) F (h) ?

59. Directions

A Tournez à gauche, puis tournez à droite. Aux feux, allez tout droit.

C Prenez la deuxième rue à droite. Aux feux, tournez à droite, et la gare est située sur votre gauche.

60. At the railway station

2 (a) 19h58 **(b)** 21h24
(c) change at Marseilles
3 (a) 16h53 **(b)** 19h01
(c) buys one-way ticket
4 (a) 18h10 **(b)** 22h42
(c) train diverted so one hour late in arriving

61. Transport

(a) a little
(b) bikes
(c) on the bus

62. Travelling

(a) There was a long queue at the motorway toll because there had been a heavy fall of snow during the night. She had to wait 20 minutes.
(b) The flight was delayed by two hours. The cafés weren't open so she had nothing to eat or drink.
(c) The man next to her snored. She wasn't able to read her book in peace.

64. Environmental issues

(a) supermarket packaging (of vegetables and fruit)
(b) people use their cars too much
(c) *two of:* traffic jams, pollution, global warming
(d) public transport, cycle lanes, pedestrian zones

66. News headlines

(a) F
(b) F
(c) ?
(d) F

Work and education

68. Opinions of school

(b) N **(c)** D **(d)** A **(e)** D

71. Primary school

(a) They were enthusiastic / more interested. Because the work wasn't hard / there was no homework.
(b) They weren't strict so the children had more fun.
(c) He wants to be a primary school teacher. It's a really fun environment.

72. Rules at school

2 E **3** C **4** D

73. Problems at school

2 C **3** H **4** A **5** E
6 G

75. Future plans

Lola: C Yanis: E Éva: F Maël: A

76. Jobs

(a) He's always tired. His hours are too long.
(b) She's a gardener.
(c) She likes it because she works outdoors.
(d) work in an office
(e) She's a writer. She works at home.
(f) Sometimes 2 hours a day and sometimes 12 hours a day.
(g) It's hard to be creative all the time.

77. Job adverts

1 B **2** C **3** C **4** B

79. Job application

(a) T **(b)** F **(c)** ?
(d) F **(e)** T

80. Job interview

(a) She's 18. / She's just turned 18.
(b) She's just taken her A levels.
(c) She plays football with her two little brothers and babysits them.
(d) *two of:* calm, strict if necessary, lots of patience
(e) She's available immediately.

81. Opinions about jobs

(a) Z **(b)** L **(c)** N **(d)** L
(e) Z **(f)** N

84. My work experience

1 N **2** P/N

Grammar

85. Articles 1

le garçon **la** mère
les étudiants **le** printemps
l'Espagne **la** Loire
la condition **le** bleu
la décision **le** père
le garage **la** plage

86. Articles 2

1 (a) Allez au
(b) Allez aux
(c) Allez à la
(d) Allez à l'
(e) Allez aux
(f) Allez au
(g) Allez au
(h) Allez à la

2 (a) Je veux du pain.
(b) Avez-vous du lait?
(c) Il n'a pas d'essence.
(d) Je vais á l'école.
(e) Est-ce que tu vas à la mairie?
(f) Il va aux toilettes.

87. Adjectives

1 un petit chien noir
2 la semaine dernière
3 Mon petit frère est très actif.
4 Ma meilleure amie est petite et timide.
5 Son frère est grand, sportif mais un peu sérieux.

88. Possessives

mon frère   ses amis
son ami   son portable
ses amis   mes parents
son sac   leur ami
ma sœur   leurs amis
son amie   leur voiture

89. Comparisons

1 L'Everest est la montagne **la plus haute** du monde.
2 La veste est **plus chère** que la robe.
3 Demain il fera **plus beau** qu'aujourd'hui.
4 **La meilleure** solution est de prendre le train.

5 Julie est **moins intelligente** que Fabien.

6 Le TGV est le train **le plus rapide.**

90. Other adjectives

1 Noé veut cette veste.
Laquelle?
Celle-ci.

2 Je préfère ce portable.
Lequel?
Celui-ci.

3 Manon a choisi ces chaussures.
Lesquelles?
Celles-ci.

4 Son frère achète ces jeux.
Lesquels?
Ceux-là.

5 On regarde ce film ce soir.
Lequel?
Celui-là

91. Adverbs

(possible answer)
Notre chat a disparu. **D'habitude,** il rentre chaque soir, **toujours** vers six heures. **Soudain,** j'ai entendu un bruit. **Très doucement** j'ai ouvert la porte et j'ai été **vraiment** surpris de voir Max avec trois petits chatons! **Finalement,** Il est entré dans la maison. **Évidemment,** Max n'est plus Max, mais Maxine!

92. Object pronouns

1 Il l'a envoyé.
2 Je ne l'ai pas regardée.
3 Il ne les a pas achetées.
4 Tu l'as vu?
5 Sarah l'a lu.
6 Mes parents l'ont achetée.

93. More pronouns: y and en

1 J'**y** suis déjà allé.
2 J'**en** ai déjà mangé trop.
3 J'**y** suis allé hier.
4 J'**y** vais de temps en temps.
5 On **y** va souvent.
6 Je n'**en** mange jamais.

94. Other pronouns

1 Mon ami **qui** s'appelle Bruno est fana de football.
2 L'émission **que** j'ai vue hier n'était pas passionnante.

3 Le quartier **où** ils habitent est vraiment calme.
4 Le prof **dont** je vous ai déjà parlé.
5 Elle a une sœur **qui** est prof.
6 J'ai accepté le stage **que** mon prof m'a proposé.

95. Present tense: -ER verbs

Je **m'appelle** Lou. J'ai une sœur qui **s'appelle** Marina et qui **joue** au tennis. Je **préfère** faire de la danse. Je **chante** et je **joue** de la guitare. Le soir nous **rentrons** à cinq heures et nous **mangeons** un casse-croûte. Puis je **tchate** avec mes amis, et j'**écoute** de la musique. Quelquefois mon frère et moi **jouons** aux jeux vidéo ou **téléchargeons** un film pour regarder plus tard.

96. -IR and -RE verbs

1 Le matin je **sors** à sept heures et demie.
2 Le mardi les cours **finissent** à cinq heures.
3 Mon copain et moi ne **buvons** pas de coca.
4 Le train **part** à 8h20.
5 Nous **apprenons** l'espagnol.
6 Pendant les vacances nous **dormons** sous la tente.
7 Mes copains **choisissent** des frites.

97. avoir and être

1 Nous **avons** un petit chaton. Il est tout noir mais il **a** les yeux verts. Il **a** toujours faim. Il **a** beaucoup de jouets mais j'**ai** une balle de ping pong qu'il adore et mon petit frère **a** un petit oiseau en fourrure qu'il déchire. **As**-tu un animal?
2 Je **suis** britannique. Je **suis** né en Angleterre. Mes parents **sont** italiens. Ils **sont** nés en Italie mais ils habitent ici depuis vingt ans. Mon frère **est** sportif. Il **est** champion régional de judo. Ma sœur **est** paresseuse. En revanche je **suis** charmant!

98. aller and faire

1 (a) Je **vais** au collège à huit heures.
(b) Nous y **allons** en car de ramassage.
(c) Le soir, on **va** au centre de sports.
(d) Ma sœur **va** à la piscine et moi, je **vais** au gymnase.
(e) Mes parents **vont** au bar, avec les autres parents!

(a) I go to school at 8 o'clock.
(b) We go in the school bus.
(c) In the evening we go to the sports centre.
(d) My sister goes to the swimming pool and I go to the gymnasium.
(e) My parents go to the bar with the other parents!

2 En hiver je **fais** du ski. Mon frère **fait** du surf et mes parents **font** aussi du ski. Ma sœur ne **fait** pas de ski mais nous **faisons** du patinage ensemble. Que **faites**-vous? In winter I go skiing. My brother goes surfing and my parents also go skiing. My sister doesn't ski but we go skating together. What do you do?

99. Modal verbs

1 (a) Martin veut y aller mais il ne peut pas.
(b) Nous voulons y aller mais nous ne pouvons pas.
(c) Vous voulez y aller mais vous ne pouvez pas.
(d) Mes parents veulent y aller mais ils ne peuvent pas.

2 (a) Je dois faire mes devoirs.
(b) Je ne sais pas faire les maths.
(c) Sais-tu faire le français?
(d) On doit apprendre les verbes.
(e) Mes copains français doivent écrire une dissertation.
(f) Je ne dois pas écrire de dissertation – je ne dois que répondre aux questions.

100. Reflexive verbs

Je ne **m'entends** pas bien avec mon grand frère. Il **se moque** de moi. Nous **nous disputons** souvent. Je **m'entends** mieux avec ma sœur. On **s'amuse** bien ensemble. Nous **nous couchons** de bonne heure parce que le matin nous **nous levons** à six heures – nous – c'est-à-dire toute la famille sauf mon frère qui ne **se réveille** pas. Quand finalement il **se lève** il ne **se douche** pas parce qu'il n'a pas le temps.

101. The perfect tense 1

Mercredi dernier **j'ai pris** le bus pour aller en ville. J'y **ai rencontré** un ami. Nous **avons fait** les magasins. J'**ai voulu** acheter des baskets rouges mais elles étaient trop chères. Nous **avons mangé** des burgers et comme boisson j'**ai choisi** un coca. Mon copain **a bu** un milkshake fraise. J'**ai laissé** mon sac au bar. Je devais y retourner mais par conséquent j'**ai raté** le bus et j'**ai dû** rentrer à pied.

102. The perfect tense 2

1 Samedi dernier je **me suis levé(e)** de bonne heure.
2 Le matin je **suis allé(e)** jouer au football.
3 Je **suis sorti(e)** à dix heures.
4 L'autre équipe **n'est pas venue**.
5 Nous y **sommes resté(e)s** une heure, puis nous **sommes rentré(e)s**.
6 Je **suis arrivé(e)** à la maison juste avant midi.

103. The imperfect tense

It's written in the imperfect because it's about what someone used to do.

Quand j'**étais** jeune, j'**habitais** à la campagne. Nous **avions** un grand jardin où je **jouais** au foot avec mes frères. Le samedi on **allait** au marché en ville. Il y **avait** beaucoup de vendeurs de fruits et légumes et un kiosque à journaux où j'**achetais** des bonbons. Nous **mangions** des merguez (des saucisses épicées) et nous **buvions** du coca. On **rentrait** en bus avec tous nos voisins et nos achats!

104. The future tense

L'année prochaine nous **irons** en France. Nous **prendrons** l'Eurostar. On **partira** de Londres et on **arrivera** à Paris. Puis on **changera** de train et on **continuera** vers le sud. Nous **ferons** du camping. Mes parents **dormiront** dans une caravane mais je **dormirai** sous une tente. Pendant la journée nous **irons** sur la plage et **jouerons** au basket et au tennis. Le soir on **mangera** au resto. On **se fera** des amis.

105. The conditional

1 Je **voudrais** aller en Italie.
2 Si j'avais assez d'argent, j'**irais** en Inde.
3 Nous **pourrions** faire un long voyage.
4 Tu **aimerais** voir ce film?
5 Je **préférerais** manger au restaurant.
6 Si j'avais faim, je **mangerais** une pizza.
7 Il **voudrait** aller en ville samedi.
8 On **pourrait** aller à la patinoire cet après-midi?
9 Tu **verrais** le match si tu restais encore deux jours.
10 Vous **voudriez** quelque chose à boire?

106. The pluperfect tense

pluperfect verbs: 1–6

imperfect verbs: 7, 11

perfect verbs: 8, 9, 10

107. Negatives

1 h **2** f **3** b **4** a **5** c **6** e **7** d **8** g

(a) Tu ne fais rien.
(b) Tu ne m'as jamais aidé à la maison.
(c) Tu ne fais plus tes devoirs.
(d) Tu ne respectes personne.
(e) Tu ne fais que le nécessaire.
(f) Tu ne peux aller ni au football ni au restaurant ce soir.

108. Questions

Où travaille ton père? Where does your father work?

Qui va à la fête? Who is going to the party?

Comment allez-vous? How are you?

Combien d'amis as-tu sur Facebook? How many friends do you have on Facebook?

À quelle heure rentrent tes parents? What time are your parents coming home?

Pourquoi as-tu raté le bus? Why did you miss the bus?

Que voulez-vous faire? What do you want to do?

Depuis quand apprends-tu le français? How long have you been learning French?

109. Useful little words

(possible answers)

1 partout
2 sous
3 dans
4 derrière
5 puis
6 dehors
7 dans
8 sans
9 à la fin
10 dans
11 au
12 sous

Your own notes

Published by Pearson Education Limited, Edinburgh Gate, Harlow, Essex, CM20 2JE.

www.pearsonschoolsandfecolleges.co.uk

Text © Pearson Education Limited 2013
Audio recorded at Tom Dick + Debbie Productions, © Pearson Education Limited
MFL Series Editor Julie Green
Edited by Pat Dunn and Sue Chapple
Typeset by Kamae Design, Oxford
Original illustrations © Pearson Education Limited 2013
Illustrations by KJA Artists
Cover illustration by Miriam Sturdee

The rights of Julie Green and Harriette Lanzer to be identified as authors of this work have been asserted by them in accordance with the Copyright, Designs and Patents Act 1988.

First published 2013

16 15 14 13
10 9 8 7 6 5 4 3 2

British Library Cataloguing in Publication Data
A catalogue record for this book is available from the British Library

ISBN 978 1 447 94102 6

Printed and bound by L.E.G.O. S.p.A. Lavis (TN) - Italy

Acknowledgements
The publisher would like to thank the following for their kind permission to reproduce their photographs:

(Key: b-bottom; c-centre; l-left; r-right; t-top)

Alamy Images: Ange 64, 125r, Blend Images 84r, Brand X. Pictures 73, Chris `Rout 84, Directphoto.org 105l, Eric Audras 65r, Geoffrey Robinson 25, Justin Kase z07z 29, Leonid Nyshko 88/2, Peter Stone 56l, Photos12 24, Pixoi Ltd 81l, 112l, Sami Sarkis 18, 118bc, Stefano Lunardi 36; **Corbis:** Image Source 98; **Creatas:** 63, 66l; **Fotolia.com:** Alexi TAUZIN 52t, Dimitri Surkov 15b, Edyta Pawlowska 15t, Rob Byron 65l, Somwaya 17, 118br; **Getty Images:** Handout 66r; **Grand Canyon National Park:** 96; **Images of France:** 103; **Imagestate Media:** John Foxx Collection 22; **iStockphoto:** Brian Pamphilon 94, Jitalia17 88/4, Mark Hatfield 83t, Teewara Soontam 88/3; **Masterfile UK Ltd:** Classic Stock 89; **MIXA Co Ltd:** 44; **Pearson Education Ltd:** Sophie Bluy 26, 69, 70, 81r, 86, 87/1, 87/2, 104, 106, 112r, Jules Selmes 43, 101, Sozaijiten 108; **PhotoDisc:** 5, Photolink 52cl; **Photolibrary.com:** Stockbroker 105; **Rex Features:** Nils Jorgensen 4; **Robert Harding World Imagery:** Ellen Rooney 94/1; **Shutterstock.com:** catwalker 35, EdBockStock 3, Gemenacom 88, Gregory Gerber 93/3, joesive47 34, Maxim Blinkov 39, Maxisport 93, Michael Cattle 62, Monkey Business images 80b, 90, Nikonaft 79, Ortodox 93/d, Paul Cowan 10, PhotoBarmley 37t, prochasson frederic 83r, Przemyslaw Ceynowa 88/6, Sergey Khakimullin 78, Shebeko 93/2, SnowWhiteImages 3r, Sorbis 45, Sue McDonald 97, Valentyn Volkov 13, 116, Vovan 88/5; **Veer/Corbis:** alexraths 80t, Andreas Karelias 55t, brykaylo 37b, erierika 58l, 112bl, fivepointsix 47b, forsterforest 56r, 125, Jonathan Larsen 52cr, martinan 55b, Monkey Business Images 58r, Pablo Scapinachis Armstrong 47t, Scirocco340 52b, sorymur 16, 118bl

All other images © Pearson Education Limited

Every effort has been made to contact copyright holders of material reproduced in this book. Any omissions will be rectified in subsequent printings if notice is given to the publishers.

In the writing of this book, no AQA examiners authored sections relevant to examination papers for which they have responsibility.